Gonder Ceramic Arts

A Comprehensive Guide

James R. Boshears &
Carol Sumilas Boshears

4880 Lower Valley Road, Atglen, PA 19310 USA

Dedication

We would like to dedicate this book and show our sincerest appreciation to Regina Brown. For the last twenty years plus, Regina, with her husband Allen at her side, collected and cherished Gonder pottery long before any of us knew what this wonderful pottery was. Not only did she collect, but also she tirelessly and accurately kept a record of mold numbers and descriptions, which have proved invaluable in doing this book. Without her knowledge, openness to share that knowledge, and motivation, this book would not be as complete as it is. Bravo Regina, bravo!

Copyright © 2001 by James R. Boshears & Carol Sumilas Boshears
Library of Congress Card Number: 2001086202

Designed by John P. Cheek
Type set in Zapf Chancery Bd BT/Zapf Humanist BT

ISBN: 0-7643-1323-1
Printed in China
1 2 3 4

Published by Schiffer Publishing Ltd.
4880 Lower Valley Road
Atglen, PA 19310
Phone: (610) 593-1777; Fax: (610) 593-2002
E-mail: Schifferbk@aol.com
Please visit our web site catalog at
www.schifferbooks.com
We are always looking for people to write books on new and related subjects. If you have an idea for a book please contact us at the above address.

This book may be purchased from the publisher.
Include $3.95 for shipping.
Please try your bookstore first.
You may write for a free catalog.

In Europe, Schiffer books are distributed by
Bushwood Books
6 Marksbury Ave.
Kew Gardens
Surrey TW9 4JF England
Phone: 44 (0)20-8392-8585
Fax: 44 (0)20-8392-9876
E-mail: Bushwd@aol.com
Free postage in the UK. Europe: air mail at cost

Contents

Acknowledgments

The authors express their sincere thanks to everyone who contributed to this collection of facts and permitted examination and photographing of their collections and other materials. To the following we owe deepest gratitude: Bernice and Ralph Baker; Jean Dieux; Diana Hansen; Charles, Joan, and Bobby Joray; Gerald Smith; P.J. Watson; and Kay Gonder Nagi (Lawton Gonder's daughter).

A very special acknowledgment is made to Regina and Allen Brown, for their constant encouragement, guidance, and tolerance of late night telephone calls, and for Regina's wisdom and knowledge of Gonder. This would not have happened without you.

A very special thanks to Rodney Emlet, who endured two visits for photographing one of the most extensive collections of Gonder we have seen.

A special credit is given to Ron and Alma Hoopes, whose knowledge of Gonder Ceramic Arts, and whose collection of catalog pages made this entire project more valid.

To Tom and Dixie Woodward, whose open house and open knowledge of Lawton Gonder and his factory, gained from Tom Woodward, Sr., made this book a joy to assemble. Their collection of experimental pieces added an insurmountable volume of knowledge to this book. Thank you for giving fellow collectors a view of what could have been.

Credit must be given to Jim and Pat Persinger, whose Gonder Museum web site has raised the awareness level of this pottery, brought additional collectors to Gonder, increased the number of pictures submitted for the book, and increased this books anticipated arrival with both present and future collectors. Thank you both very much.

We express our thanks to a special friend, Carol Le Blanc, whose constant excitement about our project kept us excited about doing it, and to her mechanics, especially Joe Neckerman, whose constant repairing of our vehicles kept us on the road to gather all of the material we did.

To the Zanesville Art Center, its Director, Philip Alan LaDouceur, and especially to Carla Kelly, for opening the boundaries of Lawton Gonder's work by allowing a yearly exhibit of Gonder Ceramic Arts, a special thanks. Their encouragement has increased the numbers of Gonder enthusiasts and opened the door for this book.

And to our son, Daryl J. Boshears, who we love to no end, and whose baby-sitting of our greyhound and cats gave us the time to go and photograph, meet with other collectors, and simply have some time to ourselves, we can never express our full thanks. But we want to state it anyway, thank you so much son. Your excitement keeps us going.

Introduction

This book has been a project of love. A love for Gonder Ceramic Arts, and the man who created this beautiful art pottery. It started when we found out that the only other book written on Gonder was not going to be expanded, updated, or reprinted. There was a distinct need for another guide, since so many pieces of Gonder had appeared in the years since the previous publication was issued in 1992.

As editors and publishers of *The Gonder Collector*, the newsletter of Gonder collectors, we had developed a lot of knowledge about the pottery and the man who created it. We also knew who had extensive collections and had the access to photograph those collections.

Over two years ago, we agreed to start photographing those collections for a possible book, at some time in the future. We did not know, at that time, where that would take us, but our wish to learn more about Gonder led us to discover even more information about this Zanesville, Ohio, company. It is this information we will share with you within the pages of this guide.

Interest in Gonder Ceramic Arts has been increasing over the last few years. We find it interesting that within the last year, both the numbers offered and the prices realized for Gonder pieces have more than doubled over those of five years ago. We have photographed many collections of Gonder pottery and have included catalog sheets to expand the coverage of this book.

Introduction

It is with great pride we present the new styling and glazing treatments introduced in this catalogue.

The Gonder Sovereign Line of vitrified china accessories was developed with colored bodies, which insures uniform coloring. Among its many virtues, the greatest is its high resistance to chipping in comparison with many china bodies now being used.

The styling of our contemporary line has been motivated by an earnest desire to combine utility, style and good craftsmanship in things of today. The work of the designers of this group reflects today's world, —sometimes vigorous, sometimes subdued.

The models of the typed art, such as animals, etc., were executed and designed by outstanding modelers in their special field.

The pieces in the Chinese line being introduced are authentic reproductions of the finest museum type and this is the first time this work has been successfully accomplished by an American manufacturer. The celadons, ming yellow and ming blue glazing treatments used on these Chinese pieces are the results of many years research and development.

Our Chinese crackle is outstanding in its texture and crystal clearness, with both of which qualities the better of the Chinese pieces have always been identified. Never before has it been possible to obtain these distinct characteristics in Chinese styling at moderate prices. It is the type of art which enhances interior decoration from early period to ultra modern.

The two new glazing treatments, gold lustre and gold antique, are new developments and are unique in the ceramic field. This is the first time a permanent gold lustre finish has been manufactured which will definitely resist the effects of body acid or abrasion. Its lustre will *not* wear off. The antique gold, with its rich brown background, is a masterpiece of research development.

Gonder ware is the art pottery made by skilled craftsmen under the supervision of a personnel with a background of three generations of pottery craftsmanship and experience. It is the sole thought and purpose of these craftsmen to produce art pottery which will be respected and appreciated by those who desire to possess the finer things in styling, craftsmanship and glazing treatments,— personifying the best in ceramic art.

The catalog sheets do not elaborate on glaze colors, sizes issued, or descriptive names. However, Gonder was specific about attaching a mold number to most pieces they produced. This mold number can be either a straight number or a combination of a letter followed by a number (ex. 101, H-73, etc.). However, it was not unusual to find two or more pieces using the same mold number; so, collectors must watch and know the description along with the mold number. Also, Gonder has used different mold numbers for what appears to be the same piece of pottery (ex. 629 and H-29, or E-65 and E-365). This can lead to confusion, and usually does. Where we have found such duplication, we have annotated each piece with the other mold numbers used.

We have included a descriptive name for each piece and measurements of the height (H), width (W), and length (L), if available. We have also tried to include the specific markings found on each piece, and identified those markings as done in block lettering (Block) or script lettering (Script) where the Gonder name is impressed or raised. This is important, since the block form of lettering was extensively used during the early production of Gonder, and especially on the molds used that previously were producing RumRill Pottery. As Gonder increased production, they hired designers to create pottery more in line with the owner's visions of art pottery. At that point, they changed the name to a script form of marking, and in many cases, added the word "Original" to the marking. The story of the RumRill and Gonder connection is explored in more depth in the history of the company.

The continuous tunnel kiln at Gonder Ceramic Arts, ready to fire what appear to be lamp bases.

A display case in the Sales Room at the factory, showing products for sale. See how many you can identify.

The pottery pieces displayed in this guide have been valued by combining prices realized at auction with prices seen and recorded at antique stores, flea markets, and private sales. We have asked several serious collectors, in various areas of the country, to review these values and make any adjustments they felt were necessary. Those changes in the values were then combined with other changes, put into a computer, and a value range from low to high was established. For those pieces that are so rare, or scarce, that not enough have entered the market to determine a fair market value, we have used a value of $N/P. This stands for "No Price," and collectors should consider the best negotiated value if they attempt to purchase such a piece.

The values set into this guide are for pieces in mint condition. Any damage, glaze variations, or the like could either increase or decrease those values. Remember, these values are estimates only. A true value is always what a seller is willing to sell for and a buyer is willing to pay for each piece. Certain glaze colors have consistently shown a premium value over common glazes. Values listed in the book are based on common glazes. Collectors should increase those values by the following percents if they find a piece in the following glaze colors: Antique Gold Crackle, +70%; Red Flambé, +50%; Turquoise Chinese Crackle, +40%; and, White Chinese Crackle, +30%. Of course, very unusual glaze combinations may also increase value.

The book is arranged by alphabetical order of subject (ex. Ashtrays, Banks, etc.). Within those categories, each piece

is then listed in order of its mold number, if known, with numbers listed first, followed by the mold numbers combining letters and numbers. Those pieces for which we have not been able to identify a mold number would be listed at the end of the subject category (with mold numbers of #N/A, None Available), in alphabetical order by their descriptive name. A mold number index is listed in the back of the book, to assist in finding the page of a known piece.

At the end of the book is a listing of those known mold numbers for which we have not been able to secure a picture. In most cases, these pieces are elusive and were not in the collections we were able to photograph. If anyone has one of these pieces, we would appreciate being notified. Hopefully, we will be able to secure a photograph of the piece for future updates of this book.

We hope that the readers of this book enjoy gazing through its pages. We have tried to provide surprises throughout, and know that there will be something for even the most serious collector. Not every collector has ever been able to track down every piece of Gonder, though some are still trying. There are some pieces that defy finding. How many Mermaid Planters are out there? What will be the defining piece in your collection? If it is not there yet, perhaps you will find it within the pages of this book, and begin the serious search for that piece. We wish you luck in that pursuit, and we continue with you in discovering the larger beauty of Gonder Ceramic Arts.

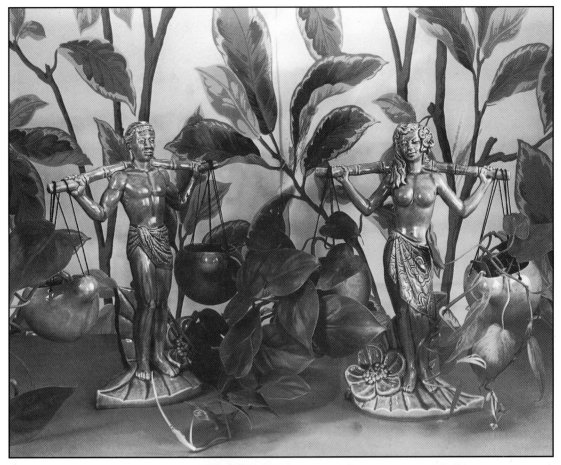

Right: An advertising display used for the Bali Planters. Note that this display photo shows the woman with no top, signifying this as a first design run. The woman was later pulled and replaced with one designed with a top.

Bottom right: Another advertising photo displaying various pieces of Gonder. Note the cigar ashtray on the top right of the table, a very hard piece to find.

Glaze Colors

We can say many things about the glazes and colors of Gonder Ceramic Arts. Ones that come to mind are beautiful, eye-catching, and even spectacular. But one thing we can be sure of, matching some of the names to the actual colors has been a somewhat difficult task.

Gonder produced a number of glazes, many of which have not been specifically identified. We have attempted to attach glaze colors to each piece presented. Those glaze colors so named have been derived from reference sources, color pictures we have been able to obtain, and the assistance of other collectors. In some cases, a glaze color has been picked for a piece that is not on the lists we have found of Gonder glazes. This color was chosen as one that most closely seems to identify a piece in the common terms of today's collectors. For example, the glaze used extensively on various pieces, combining a yellowish glaze with brown overtones, we have named "Dijon," since that color is recognized by most of today's collectors. The greenish blue mixed with the brown we call sea swirl. Red Flambé, one of the collectors' favorites, has carried that name for many years and it is believed to be the actual name for this color. There may be other flambé glazes, too.

Here we have a list, which may or may not be complete, of the various colors Gonder used. The very obvious ones, of course, are ones such as the crackle glazes: white Chinese crackle, turquoise Chinese crackle, etc. However, when it comes to the others, there is a bit of confusion. After seeing and photographing a large number of pieces, we have come to recognize what we think are some of the other more confusing glazes. For instance, we have distinguished pistachio, rutile green, Ming yellow, and coral lustre, to name a few. The other colors seem to give most collectors difficulty. We cannot seem to decide exactly which is which.

The Gonder plant identified glaze colors by number, not by color. Mr. Ron Hoopes, a long-time Gonder collector, found a listing of glaze colors, with names only, and with the help of two former Gonder employees he knew, was able to assign numbers to some of the glazes. The numbers with asterisks are identified Gonder numbers.

Various pieces of Gonder. The three pieces in the front row are all in the very hard to find category, as well as the chair planter held by the two women.

These names are:

1. Victorian Wine	14. Terra Cotta
2. Chartreuse	15. Wheat
3. White	16. French Lilac
4. Dove Gray	17. Jade
5. Blonde	18. Royal Blue
6. Black	19. Cocoa
7. Gunmetal Black	20. Pistachio
8. Gunmetal Green	21. Rosewood
9. Rosette	22. Pebble
10. Rutile Green	
11. Forest Green	
12. Sand	
13. Green Agate	

Assigned numbers:

*24. Mother of Pearl
*25. Shell Pink / Coral Lustre
*26. White Chinese Crackle
*27. Turquoise Chinese Crackle
*28. Ebony Green
*29. Royal Purple
*30. Wine Brown
*40. Antique Gold
*41. Gold Lustre
*43. Ming Yellow
*44. Celadon Green
*45. Ivory White
*46. Nubian Black

Whatever the final result of color identification, only time will tell if true knowledge of each color glaze used is finally determined. It will take the help of fellow collectors and, hopefully, former workers at Gonder, to clear the muddy waters of the glaze mystery.

History of Gonder Ceramic Arts, Inc.

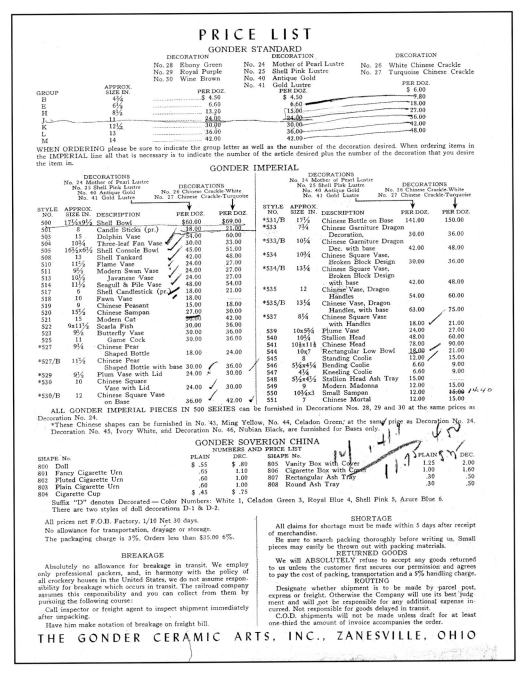

A Gonder Standard Price List sent to clients. As you can see from the prices quoted, we should have bought Gonder when it was made.

The history of Gonder Ceramic Arts is coupled with another pottery in the Zanesville, Ohio, area. In 1897, Peters and Reed was established when John Peters and Adam Reed rented the old Clark Stoneware plant in South Zanesville to make flowerpots. They were attempting to take over the customers from Sam Weller's flowerpot business, since Weller had moved to art ware. When their option came due in 1898 to purchase the building, they did not have the funds to do so. George Young purchased the building for his Roseville Pottery, where it remained a Roseville plant until it closed in 1954.

Peters and Reed purchased another building in the same area, the old South Zanesville Stoneware Company. In 1901 it was incorporated as Peters and Reed. In 1927, Harry S. McClelland bought Peters' stock; in 1921 the name of the company was changed to Zane Pottery Company. Upon Reed's death, McClelland became the sole owner. In 1931, Harry McClelland died, and his wife, Mrs. Mabel Hall McClelland, became president, and the pottery continued for another ten years. Upon her retirement, in 1941, she sold the plant to Lawton Gonder, who incorporated his company as Gonder Ceramic Arts. Gonder signed the purchase papers for the plant on December 8, 1941.

Most of the information on Lawton Gonder comes from an article written by Norris F. Schneider and published in the *Zanesville Times Signal*, Sunday, September 22, 1957. Other material comes from many other sources, including Ron Hoopes, Tom Woodward, Jr., and Kay Nagi, the daughter of Lawton Gonder.

Lawton Gonder, born August 27, 1900, in Zanesville, Ohio, grew up with the love of pottery in his blood. Both his parents worked for Sam Weller, at his Putnam, Ohio, Weller Pottery plant. The interest in pottery Gonder acquired from his parents was nourished by one of the great ceramic authorities of the country. A close neighbor of the Gonder family was John Herold, who made Chinese red ware at the Roseville Pottery and chemical porcelain at the Ohio Pottery Company. When the Gonders wanted a baby sitter for their son, they called John Herold.

A beautiful Gonder color advertisement. Do you have every piece displayed?

A young Lawton Gonder, at the beginning of his ceramic career, ready to conquer the pottery world.

At the age of 13, Lawton Gonder went to work for Herold at the Ohio Pottery Company. His job was running molds and casting handles and spouts for teapots. Gonder's admiration and respect for his first employer increased through the years. Visitors coming to Gonder's office at the South Zanesville plant were shown a water color painting by the German chemist, and were always told that Herold was a painter of glass lamp shades in Europe.

With these strong influences forming his interest in pottery, Gonder inevitably followed a career in ceramics. He started work in the Ohio Pottery at 7:00 AM, casting spouts and handles. About three hours later, Fred Laudenbacher came in and stuck the handles and spouts on the ware.

In 1915, after spending two years at the Ohio Pottery, Gonder went to work for the American Encaustic Tiling Company. At that time the great tile company was beginning the manufacture of chemical porcelain, and they needed an experienced pottery worker. World War I was in progress, and no shipments were coming from Germany, where all the chemical porcelain had been made before that period.

At American Encaustic, Gonder worked in the research department. Associated with authorities such as George It was

Stanberry, Harry Lillibridge, and Fred Rhead, Gonder was thoroughly trained in the technical and the artistic phases of ceramics. He spent 11 years in the research department.

In 1926 Gonder went to Orlando, Florida, and for one year served as general manager of that city's Cherry Art Tile Company.

In 1927, the American Encaustic Tiling Company built a new plant at Maurer, New Jersey. Gonder became the manager of that factory when it opened. There he supervised the production of the first tile for which the manufacturer issued a bond as a guarantee against crazing. This process was later used in the production of Gonder's own glaze methods.

This was called Hermosa tile. It was a trade name for the process developed by a man named Prouty at Hermosa Beach, California. American Encaustic's Superintendent, Lillibridge, bought the California plant and the patent. William McCoy was the general manager of five American Encaustic plants, including the one at Maurer. Gonder supervised the installation of the equipment for the Hermosa process there and managed the plant until 1934.

From 1934 to 1936, Gonder lived in Zanesville and acted as a consultant for the Fraunfelter China Company and the Standard Tile Company.

In 1936 he took his first step out of the tile business by becoming manager of the Florence Pottery at Mt. Giliad, Ohio. While managing the company, he processed art pottery ware for RumRill.

Being a self-taught chemist, Gonder began experimenting with applying a ceramic tile type or porcelain glaze to the pieces produced, which, up until that time were mostly done in matte glazes. Examination of the grounds around the former Mt. Giliad plant by a collector turned up numerous pieces of ceramic with a variety of glazes applied. These may have been the forerunners of the innovative glazes Gonder was to use later in producing his own pottery. When the plant burned in 1941, he decided to organize his own company in his native city.

On December 4, 1941, the following newspaper article appeared in *The Morrow County (Cardington, Ohio) Independent*:

Florence Pottery Manager to Head Zanesville Firm

Announcement of the incorporation of the Gonder Ceramic Arts, Inc. pottery to be established in South Zanesville was made last week. The company was incorporated for $95,000 with 1200 shares of stock.

Lawton Gonder, general manager of the Florence Pottery Co. at Mt. Gilead, will be the general manager of the new company. He formerly resided in Zanesville, being the superintendent of the old Fraunfelter China Co.

In the *Crockery and Glass Journal* (January 1943, p. 95), it was stated that *Gonder Ceramic Arts, Inc. made pottery for RumRill for the next year until January 1943, when Gonder announced that Gonder Ceramic Arts, Inc. would henceforth devote all its plant facilities to an art ware line to be merchandised under its own name.* Both company's catalogs from that time period show that the RumRill line became the initial Gonder line, hence many pieces show up marked both ways.

When the Gonder Ceramic Arts plant opened, many of the first pieces produced there followed the RumRill line from the Florence Pottery plant. Gonder purchased or otherwise secured the molds for his own use after George Rumrill dissolved his company. Many early pieces marked with the impressed "Gonder" block mark have been found with RumRill glaze treatments.

When other companies were turning to the production of cheaper ware for chain stores, Gonder started the manufacture of higher priced art pottery and continued to make that grade of ware after the war. Zanesville was then the home of three of the four largest art potteries in the United States during the 1940s: Weller, Roseville, and Gonder. The fourth was the Haeger Pottery at Dundee, Illinois.

For his designs, Gonder went to some of the best sculptors and artists in the country. Jamie Matchet, sculptor and designer for Gorham silver, originated some of the Gonder pieces and had a modeler do the work on his designs. Chester Kirk of Elmhurst, Illinois, who designed exhibits for the New York and Chicago World's Fairs, also created shapes. Two other Gonder designers were Helen Conover of Chicago and F.F. Greene of Westport, Connecticut.

Gonder created several artistic innovations in the ceramic field during the fifteen years he produced pottery at the South Zanesville plant. One of these was the first commercial production of flambé glazes. This glaze resembles flames, and is red with streaks of yellow color throughout the piece.

A second innovation was the creation of gold crackle, which had never been successfully done before. He stated in a Gonder catalog: "Antique Gold Crackle is the miracle of modern ceramic artistry. Long a challenge to potters, in more than two thousand years it had never before been successfully produced. Gonder pours gleaming 24-carat gold metal over the glorious symmetry of Gonder shapes, then crackles the gold with an exclusive process. Each antique gold crackle form is a true masterpiece, unique, individually yours, never duplicated."

A third accomplishment of Gonder Ceramic Arts was the development and introduction of a commercial line of Chinese crackle glazes. As also stated in a Gonder catalog: "Our Chinese crackle is outstanding in its texture and crystal clearness, with both of which qualities the better of the Chinese pieces have always been identified. Never before has it been possible to obtain these distinct characteristics in Chinese styling at moderate prices."

A fourth achievement of which Gonder was proud was the duplication of old Chinese pottery. Gonder acquired old museum pieces of Chinese potters and duplicated them.

The catalog described this line as follows: "The pieces in the Chinese line being introduced are authentic reproductions of the finest museum type, and this is the first time this work has been accomplished by an American manufacturer. The Celadon, Ming yellow and Ming blue glazing treatments used on these Chinese pieces are the result of many years research and development."

During World War II the demand for pottery was so great that it could not be met at the South Zanesville factory. Gonder bought the old Drake Lumber Company mill at 641 Lee Street, in 1946. Here he built two and three story additions, and opened a plant for the exclusive manufacture of lamp bases.

created as a separate corporation, named the Elgee Pottery, after the first two initials of the owner. Many of these lamp bases were sold to one distributor, "The Bradley Manufacturing Company" of Chicago, Illinois. Most of these lamp pieces are not marked and do not display normal Gonder glaze treatments.

The Lawt Gonder we know. Owner of Gonder Ceramic Arts and creator of art pottery.

The Elgee Pottery was destroyed by fire on May 5, 1954. Gonder built a concrete block addition to his South Zanesville plant that added 25,000 square feet of floor space, making a total of 100,000 square feet. All operations were then concentrated at the South Zanesville plant.

As the foreign importation of pottery began to hurt the business of American manufacturers, Gonder decided to use the knowledge he had acquired in many years with the American Encaustic Tiling Company. In 1955 he began to train his employees in the manufacture of tile. In February 1957, he converted his entire production to other ceramic products.

In 1957, Gonder sold his business to Allied Tile Company. He continued to work as a consultant to the Allied Tile Company for many years, but eventually retired to Largo, Florida. Lawton Gonder died on November 4, 1975, and was returned to his hometown of Zanesville, Ohio, where he was buried in Memorial Cemetery.

The name Gonder Ceramic Arts has remained relatively unknown, except to a few die hard collectors. Gonder Ceramic Arts, Inc. produced a wide variety of both functional and art pottery designs. Gonder's area of expertise was ceramic glazes. He excelled in this field so well that he was recognized by The American Ceramic Society and awarded a fellowship in the Society. This allowed him to use the title "Fellow of the American Ceramic Society."

Gonder produced an eclectic mix of art pottery and shipped it all over the United States. His designs were influenced by both Oriental art and what we term "modern deco." Shape designs used plants, animals, and the sea as natural subject matter. The animal-shaped pieces, both figurines and vases, are difficult to find, highly prized by collectors, and the most sought after pieces.

Gonder also developed the use of what he termed "Volcanic Glazes." This process involved two glazes with different chemical properties and different melting temperatures. When the piece was fired in the kiln, one glaze would actually run or melt over the other. Other potteries in the area soon copied this process on their wares.

Most Gonder pieces are marked with the name of the pottery, a mold number, and sometimes "USA." However, there are a few pieces that are not marked, or were marked with a paper label that has been removed, and Gonder collectors seek these out. Once you become accustomed to the Gonder glazes, you can usually recognized them from across a room. Many pieces have a double glaze, with a pink underglaze. These pieces almost always display pink on the interior of the piece. The only exceptions are the crackle glazes, which may display any color on the interior.

Another method used by collectors to identify unmarked pieces has been the presence of the kiln stands mark. This is a straight-line indentation on the edge of the piece where it rested while being fired in the kiln. Usually, three such lines are found, equal distances apart. However, several pieces with wider bases have been found with four such indented lines.

Some of the lamp bases have been found marked; but, when found, they are marked Gonder, not Elgee. When such lamp bases are found, they are usually pieces that were in the normal ware line produced by Gonder and were modified to serve as lamp bases. Of the others identified, identification is usually made through the glaze used and the subject matter found.

All of the lamp bases have been found to be made of a very white clay, which can be viewed inside the lamp. Usually, when glazed on the outside, some of the glaze can be seen spilled into parts of the inside of the lamp's interior prior to the firing process. This is not a verified identification, but helps in the determination of whether to consider such an item as a Gonder lamp base.

In 1972, after Gonder's retirement, a book was published entitled *Zanesville Art Tile in Color* in which items produced at Gonder Ceramic Arts were shown but no credits were given to Gonder. These items were in fact credited to other potters. This was of much concern to Lawton Gonder and he struggled to right this wrong. He died before the task was accomplished. We hope that this book and other, future publications will help by giving Lawton Gonder credit for his innovative glazes and tile designs.

A Gonder's Collector's Association was formed years ago, and publishes a quarterly newsletter. At the time of this writing, dues were $15.00 per year. The Association meets once each year, during the Zanesville Pottery Festival, in mid-July. Collector's attending bring newly discovered pieces for display during the "Show 'N Tell" portion of the meeting. Information about the Association may be received from the authors of this book.

Gonder pottery is functional and of high quality. Most pieces discovered, even today, show little wear and are in exceptional condition. Gonder's glaze treatments were so good that many pieces do not even reflect the crazing that appears on most other pottery. All in all, Gonder is a distinctive and quality art pottery. As such, this artware currently waits for collectors to discover and covet the pieces as much as those of other Ohio potteries.

Plant Manager
Thomas R. Woodward, Sr.
Biography

Thomas R. Woodward, Sr., Plant Manager/ Plant Superintendent of Gonder Ceramic Arts.

Thomas R. Woodward, Sr. was born in 1911 in Salineville, Ohio, in the heart of the pottery business in Ohio. After graduation, he worked in a number of potteries in the Wellsville and East Liverpool, Ohio, area, and Cronin China Company in Minerva, Ohio.

When discharged from the service in 1946, his relationship with Bob Hull resulted in his being hired at Hull Art Pottery in Crooksville, Ohio. In 1947, Lawton (Lawt) Gonder hired him as Plant Manager/Plant Superintendent of the Elgee Pottery located on Lee Street in Zanesville, Ohio. This started a long-standing work relationship and friendship that remained strong until Mr. Woodward's death in 1969.

In 1954, Elgee Pottery burned to the ground. Lawt transferred Mr. Woodward to his South Zanesville plant, Gonder Ceramic Arts, as a Plant Manager/ Plant Superintendent. His responsibilities included calculating color formulas, testing for color accuracy and quality production, running the chemical laboratory, purchasing the clay, talc, all ceramic chemicals, shipping to wholesale and retail outlets, hiring plant personnel, and managing the entire production process.

After Lawt Gonder sold the company to Allied Tile Company, he continued as a consultant for several years and Mr. Woodward continued as Plant Superintendent of Allied Tile Company until his death in 1969.

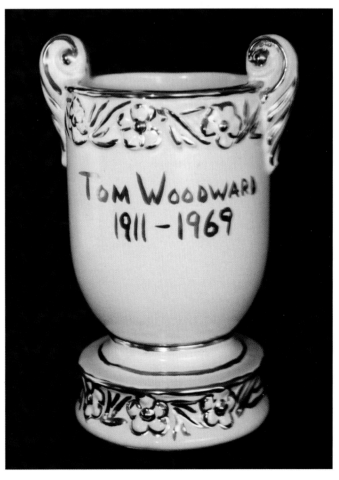

A loving cup given by the plant employees to Tom Woodward upon his retirement from Allied Tile in 1969.

Chapter 1
Sign

This chapter contains only one piece of Gonder, the elusive dealer sign. It is fitting, though, that it stands as its own chapter and as the beginning of this book. This one piece is extremely hard to find; the collector who has this one searched for years to find it. If you see this dealer sign once, and do not get it then, you may never see another one in your lifetime.

Mold #N/A, Gonder Dealer Sign. (Rare. Only 2-3 of these have been found to date. Since they were reserved for retailers of Gonder, there are not many around, and thus these signs are considered rare.) 6-1/4" L, Mark: "Gonder Pottery", Block, Forest Green. *Courtesy of Regina & Al Brown.* Value: $N/P.

Chapter 2
Ashtrays

Will we ever see the end of the Gonder ashtrays? Each day brings more and more of them to the collective consciousness. Many of the ashtrays were not marked as Gonder, since they were sold to the Bradley Manufacturing Company to be marketed under their name. Thus, one must search by glaze color to attempt recognition. Those pieces that are numbered are listed first, with the unknown numbered ones following. Please contact us if you have one of these heretofore "unnumbered" ashtrays that displays a mold number, so that it can be added to the database for all collectors.

Mold #113, Fish Ashtray with Open Mouth (very hard to find), 3-3/4"H x 4" W x 9" L, Mark: "113 Gonder Original," Script, Onionskin. *Courtesy of Regina & Al Brown.* Value: $70-90.

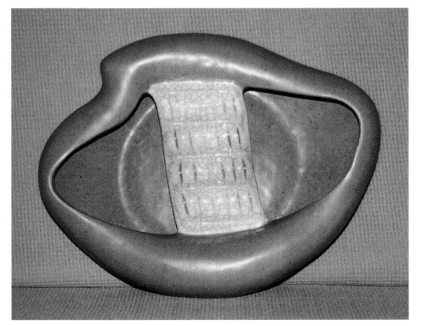

Mold #219, Center Rest Ashtray, 2-1/4" H x 7-1/2" W, Mark: "Gonder Original 219," Script, Blue with White Chinese Crackle. *Courtesy of Bernice A. & Ralph H. Baker.* Value: $50-75.

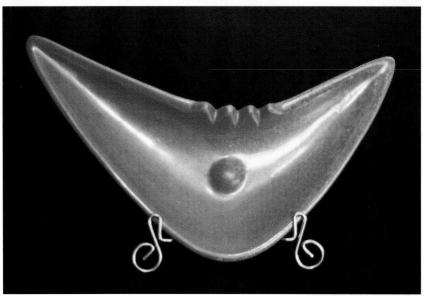

Mold #223, Boomerang Ashtray, 6-1/4" W x 10-1/2" L, Mark: "223 Gonder Original," Script, Terra Cotta. *Courtesy of Tom & Dixie Woodward.* Value: $25-40.

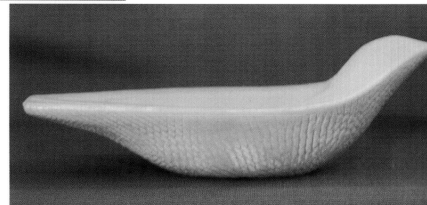

Mold #224, Bird Ashtray, 2-7/8" H x 8-7/8" L, Mark: "Gonder Original 224," Script, Chartreuse. *Courtesy of Regina & Al Brown.* Value: $25-40.

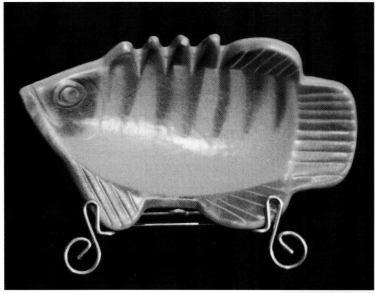

Mold #224, Spiked Fish Ashtray, 4" W x 7-3/8" L, Mark: "Gonder Original," Script, Onionskin. *Courtesy of Tom & Dixie Woodward.* Value: $40-60.

Mold #406, Ashtray Set with Cigarette Holder, 3-7/8" W x 3-7/8" L, Mark: None, Antique Gold Crackle. *Courtesy of Tom & Dixie Woodward.* Value, normally: $50-75; with this glaze: $85-125.

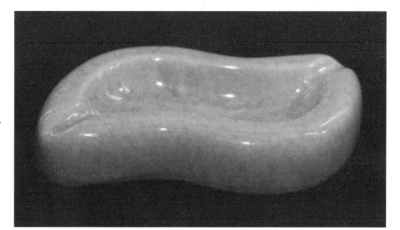

Mold #408, Art Deco Curve Ashtray, 1-3/4" H x 5" W x 10" L, Mark: None, Dove Gray. *Courtesy of Rod Emlet.* Value: $25-35.

Mold #548, Horse Head Ashtray, 6" H, Mark: None, Nubian Black with Gold Lustre (unusual glaze color). *Courtesy of Tom & Dixie Woodward.* Value: $40-60.

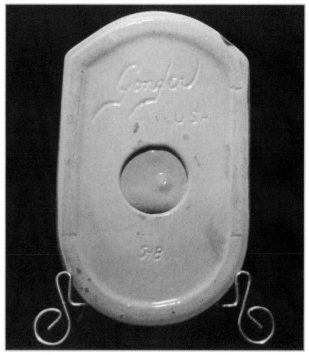

Mold #548, Horse Head Ashtray (bottom view), Mark: "Gonder USA 548," Script, Sea Swirl.

Mold #548, Horse Head Ashtray (regular view), 5-5/8" H x 4-1/4" W x 6-7/8" L, Mark: "Gonder USA 548," Script, Sea Swirl. Value: $25-50.

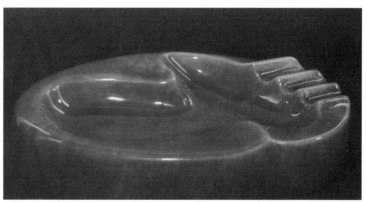

Mold #586, Foot Shaped Ashtray, 1-7/8" H x 9-1/2" W x 9-3/4" L, Mark: None, Rutile Green. *Courtesy of Rod Emlet.* Value: $20-30.

Mold #626, "S" Swirl Ashtray, 1-1/2" H x 6-1/2" W x 9-1/8" L, Mark: "626," Block, Forest Green with Volcanic Light Green Drip. Value: $20-30.

Mold #805 & #N/A, Rectangular Ashtray with Unknown Round Mug, Mark: base, "Gonder 805," & mug: None, Script, Dove Gray with Volcanic White Drip. *Courtesy of Tom & Dixie Woodward.* Value: $60-80.

Mold #805 & #909, Rectangular Ashtray with La Gonda Wavy Handle Square Mug Set (very hard to find), Mark: base: "Gonder 805," & mug: "Gonder 909," Script, Yellow with Volcanic White Drip. *Courtesy of Bernice A. & Ralph H. Baker.* Value: $50-75.

Mold #807, Round Piecrust Ashtray, 9" W, Mark: "Gonder Original," Script, Sea Swirl. *Courtesy of Regina & Al Brown.* Value: $20-40.

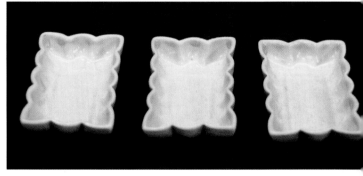

Mold #807, Sovereign Fluted Rectangular Ashtrays (3) (very hard to find), 1-7/8" W x 3-1/4" L, Mark: None, White. *Courtesy of Rod Emlet.* Value, each: $20-30.

Mold #808, Round Fluted Sovereign Ashtray Set (very hard to find), 1" H x 2-3/4" W, Mark: "Sovereign Gonder U.S.A.," Block; Pink, White, & Blue. *Courtesy of Regina & Al Brown.* Value, each: $20-30.

Mold #814, Square with Rounded Corners Ashtray, 8" W x 8" L, Mark: "Gonder Original," Script, Celadon Green Crackle. *Courtesy of Tom & Dixie Woodward.* Value, normally: $20-40; with this glaze: $30-60.

Mold #815, Square with Inside Concentric Ridges Ashtray, 2-1/2" H x 10" W x 10" L, Mark: "Gonder Original," Script, Forest Green. *Courtesy of Tom & Dixie Woodward.* Value: $25-50.

Mold #1800 A, Large Square Ashtray (hard to find), 1-1/2" H x 10-11/16" W x 10-11/16" L, Mark: "Gonder Original," Script, Black with White Swirl. *Courtesy of Tom & Dixie Woodward.* Value: $50-75.

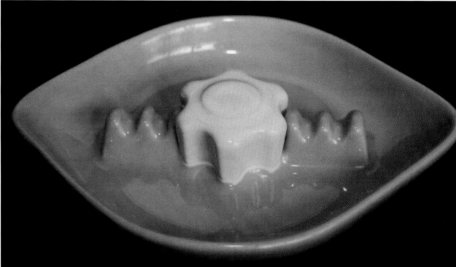

Mold #N/A, Middle Spigot Ashtray, 9-5/8" W x 7-3/4" L, Mark: None, Shell Pink. *Courtesy of Tom & Dixie Woodward.* Value: $20-40.

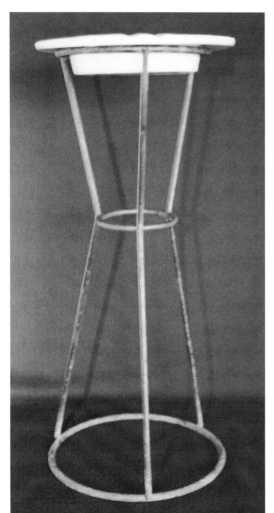

Right: Mold #N/A, Circular Ashtray from previous metal stand, 9" W, Mark: "Gonder," Script, Celadon Green Crackle. *Courtesy of Tom & Dixie Woodward.* Value, ashtray alone: $50-75.

Mold #N/A, Circular Ashtray with Metal Stand (scarce), 9" W x 20-1/4" L, Mark: "Gonder," Script, Celadon Green Crackle. *Courtesy of Tom & Dixie Woodward.* Value, normally: $100-125; with this glaze: $125-150.

Mold #N/A, Oblong Hobnail with 4-Section Center Ashtray, 1-3/4" H x 7-3/4" W x 9-1/4" L, Mark: None, Black with Yellow Crackle Center. *Courtesy of Tom & Dixie Woodward.* Value: $50-75.

Mold #N/A, Square Ashtray (imprint "PAT"), 2-1/8" H x 7-1/2" W x 7-1/2" L, Mark: None, Black. *Courtesy of Regina & Al Brown.* Value: $20-40.

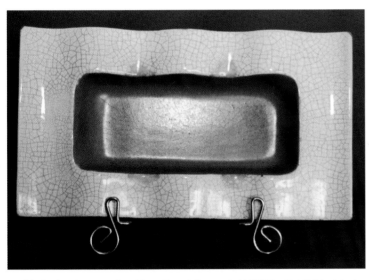

Mold #N/A, Rectangular Wavy Top Ashtray, 5-1/4" W x 9-1/4" L, Mark: "Gonder Original," Script, Chinese White Crackle with Onionskin. *Courtesy of Tom & Dixie Woodward.* Value: $30-50.

Mold #N/A, Shield with Holly Leaves & "Merry Christmas" imprint Ashtray (rare), 5-1/2" W x 5" L, Mark: None, White. *Courtesy of Tom & Dixie Woodward.* Value: $N/P.

Mold #N/A, Square Recessed Ashtray, 10-1/2" W x 10-1/2" L, Mark: None, Black with White Center. *Courtesy of Tom & Dixie Woodward.* Value: $20-40.

Mold #N/A, Double Interlocking Ashtrays (very hard to find), 4-1/4" W x 4" L, Mark: None, Black & White Chinese Crackle. *Courtesy of Tom & Dixie Woodward.* Value: $50-75.

Chapter 3
Banks, Bases, Baskets, Bells, & Bookends

This chapter groups together several pieces, since there are not enough of each to warrant separate chapters. The bases shown do not display all that exist. Some you will find in other chapters under vases or jars. These bases were specifically made to display certain vases or jars. We have shown some separate examples here, but you should watch for the others also.

Mold #950, Large Sheriff Bank, back view. (Shows coin slot on top of hat.) *Courtesy of Rod Emlet.*

Mold #950, Large Sheriff Bank, front view. (Cookie jar with top fused at factory to create a bank. This is the only example we have heard of, so this piece may be quite rare.) 10-1/2" H, Mark: None, Yellow with Black. *Courtesy of Rod Emlet.* Value: $N/P.

Mold #N/A, Small Sheriff Bank, 9-1/2" H x 7-1/8" W, Mark: "Gonder Original," Script, Yellow with Black. (This bank also was made in total green with black and with a green shirt on the sheriff. Banks with green are slightly harder to find and you would expect to see them valued slightly higher.) *Courtesy of Bernice A. & Ralph H. Baker.* Value: $350-450.

Mold #535-B, 4-Footed Base for Dragon Handle Vase Mold #535 (very hard to find), 2-1/16" H x 4-5/8" W x 5-13/16" L, Mark: "Gonder USA 535," Script, Gunmetal Black. Value: $50-75.

Mold #800, Sovereign Bonnet Lady Bell, front view (very hard to find), 3-1/2" H, Paper Label Mark: "Sovereign Gonder U.S.A.," Block, White. *Courtesy of Regina & Al Brown.* Value: $75-100.

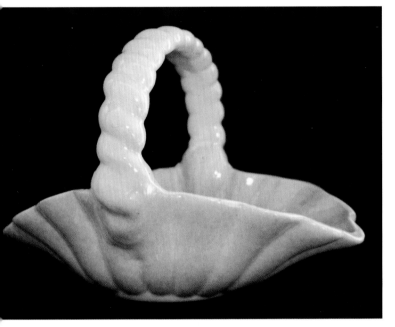

Mold #L-19 or #419, Large Fluted Basket, 8-7/8" H x 13-1/16" L, Mark: "Gonder L-19," Script, Ming Yellow. Value: $30-45.

Mold #800, Sovereign Bonnet Lady Bell (back view). *Courtesy of Regina & Al Brown.*

Mold #H-39 with RumRill Mold #H-39 (almost identical molds with slight variations between the two), Small Handle Basket with RumRill Small Handle Basket, 6-5/8" H x 8-1/4" L, Mark: "H-39 Gonder U.S.A.," Block, Celadon Green (Gonder) & Red/White (RumRill). Value, Gonder: $10-20.

Mold #211, Grecian Horse Bookends, 10" H, Paper Label Mark: "Gonder," Script, Royal Purple. *Courtesy of Bernice A. & Ralph H. Baker.* Value, Pair: $100-125.

Mold #220, Roman Horse Head Bookends, 8" H, Mark: "220 Gonder Original," Script, Pistachio. *Courtesy of Bernice A. & Ralph H. Baker.* Value: $100-150.

Mold #582, Horse Head Bookends, 9" H, Mark: None, Forest Green. *Courtesy of Regina & Al Brown.* Value: $100-125.

Chapter 4
Bowls

Bowls comprise many pieces, from console bowls used in sets with candleholders (popular in the 1950s) to planter type bowls used for holding just about anything. Even the butter warmer is, in essence, a bowl for holding and melting butter.

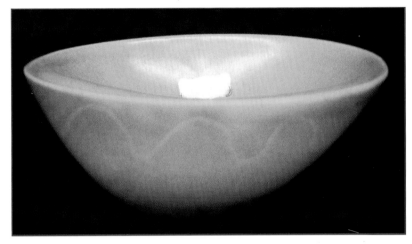

Mold #101, Divided Bowl, side view (scarce), 3-1/8" H x 9-3/8" W, Paper Gonder Label, Onionskin. *Courtesy of Regina & Al Brown.* Value: $N/P.

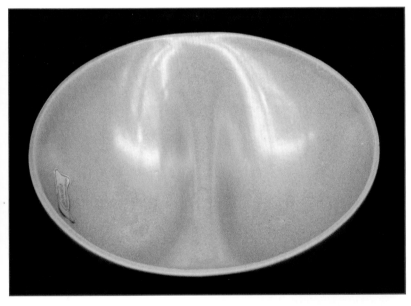

Mold #101, Divided Bowl (top view). *Courtesy of Regina & Al Brown.*

Mold #500, Large Shell Console Bowl, 4-11/16" H x 10" W x 17-1/2" L, Mark: "500 U.S.A.," Block, Coral Lustre. Value: $125-150.

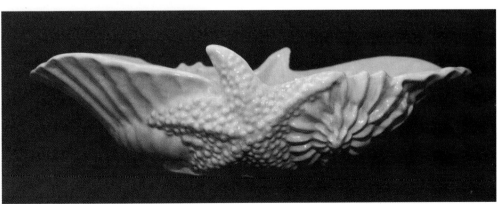

Mold #505, Seashell Console Bowl, 7-1/4" H x 5-1/4" W x 16-1/8" L, Mark: "505 Gonder U.S.A.," Block, Mother Of Pearl. *Courtesy of Regina & Al Brown.* Value: $50-65.

Mold #520 & #520/c, Freeform Console Bowl with Candleholders, bowl: 2-5/8" H x 8-7/8" W x 11-1/4" L; candleholders: 1-13/16" H x 4-1/4" W x 5-1/2" L, bowl Mark: "Gonder Original 520," candleholder Mark: "Gonder 520C," Script, Dijon. Value, bowl: $50-75; Candleholders, each: $30-35.

Mold #521, Shell Cornucopia Console Bowls (Pair), both 6-7/8" H x 12" L, marks: "Gonder Original 521," Script, left: Red Flambé, right: Dijon. Value, left: $ 35-60; right: $25-40.

Mold #523, Round Scallop Lotus Bowl, 2-1/8" H x 9-1/2" W, Mark: "Gonder Original 523," Script, White with Blue Swirl. *Courtesy of Regina & Al Brown.* Value: $35-50.

Mold #556, Console Bowl with Dolphins, 4-5/8" H x 11-1/4" L, Mark: "556 Gonder U.S.A.," Script, Ming Yellow. Value: $55-70.

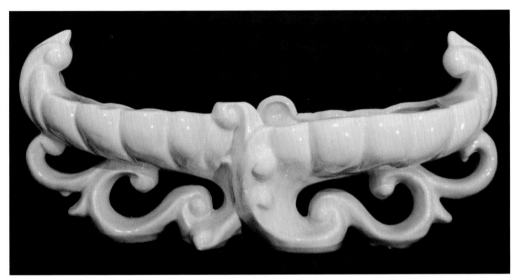

Mold #557, "Banana Boat" Console Bowl (so named by factory workers), 6-7/8" H x 15-1/4" L, Mark: "Gonder 557 USA," Script, Chartreuse. Value: $60-80.

Mold #592, "S" Shaped Bowl (side view), 2-1/2" H x 6-7/8" W x 11-7/8" L, Mark: "Gonder Original 592," Script, Butterscotch. *Courtesy of Regina & Al Brown.* Value: $20-40.

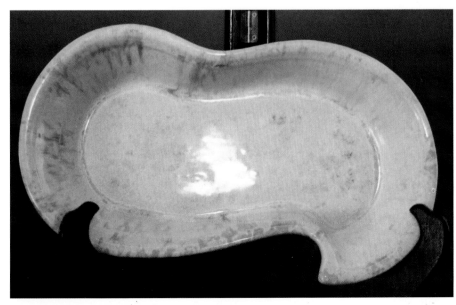

Mold #592, "S" Shaped Bowl (top view). *Courtesy of Regina & Al Brown.*

29

Mold #715, Round Flat Bowl, 2-3/8" H x 8" W, Mark: "Gonder Original 715," Script, Royal Blue with White Volcanic Drip. *Courtesy of Rod Emlet.* Value: $15-25.

Mold #996, Butter Warmer with Box, 4-1/4" H, Mark: "Gonder 996," Script, Forest Green. Value, with box: $ 35-50; without box: $25-40.

Mold #742, Hexagon with Chinese Figures Bowl, 5-1/8" H x 8-1/2" W, Mark: "742," Block, Dove Gray with White Volcanic Drip. *Courtesy of Tom & Dixie Woodward.* Value: $25-40.

Mold #2641, Oak Leaf Serving Bowl. (This is the only one of these seen to date. Scarce.) 2-3/4" H x 12-1/2" W x 15-1/2" L, Mark: "2641," Block, Onionskin. *Courtesy of Tom & Dixie Woodward.* Value: $N/P.

Mold #B 17, Small Leaves Bowl, side view (very hard to find), 1-3/8" H x 5-11/16" W, Mark: "Gonder B 17," Script, Coral Lustre. Value: $40-60.

Mold #B 17, Small Leaves Bowl, bottom view.

Mold #H-29 or #629, Large Fluted Bowl, 2-7/8" H x 8" W, Mark: "Gonder H-29 U.S.A.," Script, Sea Swirl. Value: $20-30.

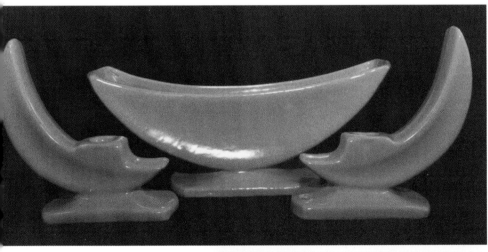

Mold, Bowl: #J-55; Candleholders: #J-56, Crescent Moon Console Bowl with Candleholders, bowl: 4-1/4" H x 5-1/4" W x 12-3/4" L; candleholders: 6-1/2" H x 6-1/4" L, console bowl Mark: "J 55;" candleholder Mark: "Gonder U.S.A. J-56," bowl: Block; candleholders: Script, Mother of Pearl. *Courtesy of Rod Emlet.* Value, as set: $75-100; bowl alone: $25-40.

Mold #J-71, Fluted with Flowers Console Bowl, 4-3/4" H x 5-1/8" W x 12-3/4" L, Mark: "J-71 Gonder U.S.A.," Script, French Lilac. Value: $50-75.

Chapter 5

Candleholders & Carafes

Gonder produced a number of candleholders, some as separate items and some as components of console sets. We are sure they were sold separately, since the number of candleholders on the market far exceeds the number of console bowls. Carafes, on the other hand, are not readily available. Since they held hot liquids, many of them were probably broken during use, and they are, subsequently, harder to find.

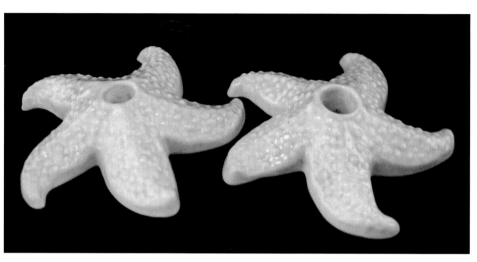

Mold #501, Starfish Candleholders. (The match for the Mold #500 Shell Console Bowl. Hard to find.) 7-7/8" W, Mark: "USA 501," Block, Mother Of Pearl. *Courtesy of Regina & Al Brown.* Value, each: $60-80.

Mold #506, Single Shell Candleholder. (Can be used with Mold #505 Shell Console Bowl.) 4-5/8" H x 2-3/4" W, Mark: "Gonder USA," Script, Coral Lustre. Value, each: $10-20.

Mold #517, Cornucopia Double Candleholders. (Shown with Mold #505 Shell Console Bowl. Hard to find.) 4" H x 3-3/4" W x 6-7/8" L, Mark: None, Sea Swirl. *Courtesy of Rod Emlet.* Value, each: $60-80.

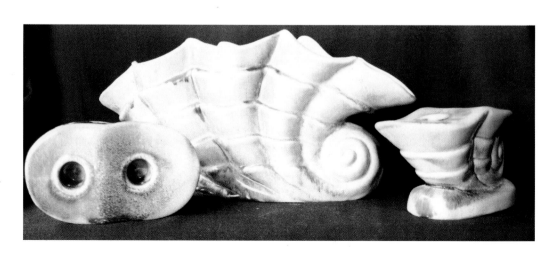

Mold #518, Triangle Bowl Candleholder (very hard to find), 12-1/2" W x 10-1/4" L, Mark: "Gonder Original 518," Script, Sea Swirl. *Courtesy of Regina & Al Brown.* Value: $100-125.

Mold #561, Dolphin Candleholders. (Usually used with Mold #H-85 Triple Dolphin Vase as a console set.) 2-1/2" H x 5" L, Mark: "Gonder U.S.A. 561," Script, Sea Swirl. *Courtesy of Regina & Al Brown.* Value, each: $40-60.

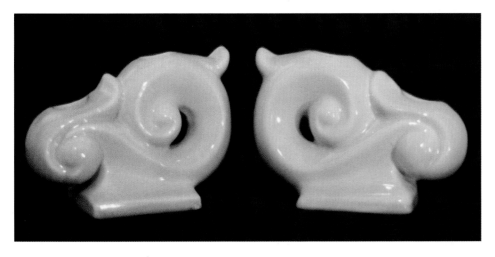

Mold #565, Curled Candleholders. (Matched with Mold #557, "Banana Boat" Console Bowl, to form a console set.) 4-1/8" H x 5-3/4" L, Mark: "Gonder 565 USA," Script, Chartreuse. Value, each: $40-50.

Mold #726, Cube Candleholder, 2-1/4" H x 3" W x 3" L, Mark: None, Chartreuse, with White Volcanic Drip. *Courtesy of Regina & Al Brown.* Value: $20-30.

Mold #521/C, Shell Candleholders (shown with Mold #521 Shell Console Bowl), 3-3/4" H x 6-1/4" L, Mark: None, Red Flambé. *Courtesy of Regina & Al Brown.* Value, normally: $25-35; with this glaze: $35-45.

Mold #N/A, Covered Gourd Candleholder (scarce), 4-3/4" H, Mark: None, Wine Brown. *Courtesy of Tom & Dixie Woodward.* Value: $N/P.

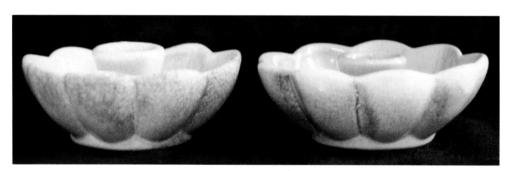

Mold #E-14 or #314 or #414, Fluted Candleholders, 1-7/8" H x 4-5/8" W, Mark: "E-14 Gonder U.S.A.," Script, Wine Brown. Value, each: $10-15.

Mold #994, Carafe with Lid & Metal Stand (very hard to find with stand), Carafe: 8" H, with stand: 12", Mark: "Gonder Original," Script, Gunmetal Black. *Courtesy of Tom & Dixie Woodward.* Value: $75-100.

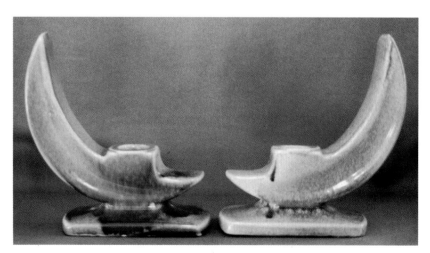

Mold #J-56, Crescent Moon Candleholder. (Used with Mold #J-55 Crescent Moon Console Bowl to form a console set.) 6-1/2" H x 6-1/4" L, Mark: "Gonder U.S.A. J-56," Script, Sea Swirl. *Courtesy of Regina & Al Brown.* Value, each: $50-60.

Chapter 6
Cookie Jars & Creamers

Gonder did not produce many cookie jars, in either style or number. All of the cookie jars are very hard to find, or downright scarce, and command premium prices when found. Since they are sought by both Gonder collectors and cookie jars collectors, we do not foresee this changing for the future. Most of the creamers produced were made for the La Gonda series, and will be found in that section (*see* chapter 12). Where we have found a stand-alone creamer, we have placed it in this section. Hopefully, more can be added to this chapter in the future.

Mold #N/A, Pirate Cookie Jar. (This jar has now been found in two heights, 12" H & the size pictured here. This cookie jar has also been reproduced, so watch for copies. Scarce.) 10-1/2" H, Mark: None, Yellow & Blue. *Courtesy of Rod Emlet.* Value: $1,500-1,800.

Mold #924, Bulb with Sleeping Dog Finial Cookie Jar, 8-1/2" H, Mark: "Gonder U.S.A.," Script, Victorian Wine with Volcanic White Drip. Value: $75-100.

Mold #P-24, Round Fluted with Round Finial Cookie Jar (Pair), 8-1/4" H, mark, both: "Gonder P-24 U.S.A.," Block, left: French Lilac, right: Ming Yellow with Brown Drip. Value, both: $15-40.

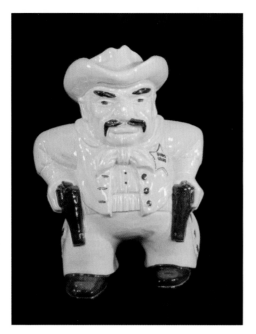

Mold #974, Ye Olde Oaken Bucket Cookie Jar. (This jar would figure to be very common, but only this one has surfaced to date; until others appear, no price can be determined, and we must consider this cookie jar as rare.) 7" H, Mark: "Gonder Original 974," Script, Brown with Tan & Yellow. *Courtesy of Ron & Alma Hoopes.* Value: N/P.

Mold #950, Sheriff Cookie Jar (very hard to find), 11-3/4" H x 8-3/4" W, Mark: "Gonder Original 950," Script, Yellow & Black (this is the more common color variation found). *Courtesy of Rod Emlet.* Value: $1,000-1,200.

Mold #974, Ye Olde Oaken Bucket Cookie Jar (bottom view). *Courtesy of Ron & Alma Hoopes.*

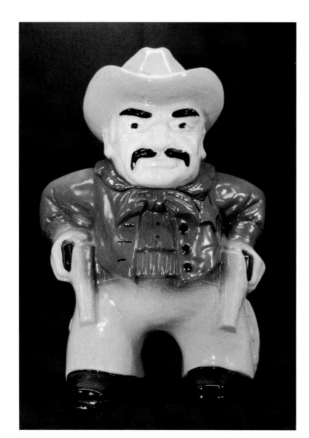

Mold #404, Squashed Creamer, 7" H, Mark: "Gonder 404," Script, White. *Courtesy of Charles Joray.* Value: $25-40.

Mold #950, Sheriff Cookie Jar (very hard to find), 11-3/4" H x 8-3/4" W, Mark: "Gonder Original 950," Script, Yellow with Green Top, & Black (this color variation is harder to find than the solid yellow with black feet). *Courtesy of Rod Emlet.* Value: $1,200-1,400.

Chapter 7
Dishes

One of the first surprises we found when photographing this chapter was that Gonder produced two different sizes of the six-section relish dish (called the amoebae dish by many collectors). Prior to this, many thought only one size was made, but two different sizes, with the same mold number, have been found and verified. The Oak Leaf dish displayed was a previously unknown piece, but is definitely a Gonder dish. Will other pieces be found? Only time will tell.

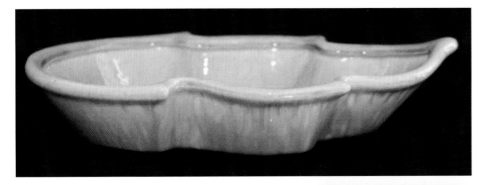

Mold #591, Oak Leaf Dish (side view), 2-9/16" H x 8-1/16" W x 12-13/16" L, Mark: "Gonder Original 591," Script, Dijon. Value: $40-60.

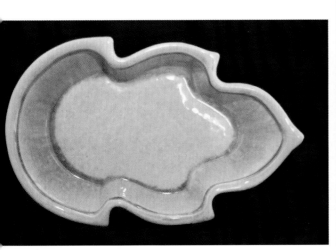

Mold #591, Oak Leaf Dish (top view).

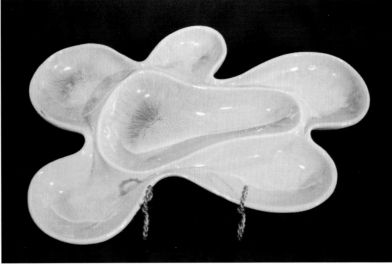

Mold #871, Large Six Section Relish Dish (not easy to find), 1-1/2" H x 11-1/8" W x 18-5/8" L, Mark: "Gonder Original 871," Script, Dijon. Value: $125-150.

Mold #871, Small Six Section Relish Dish. (This was previously thought to have been produced in only one size — large, until this second smaller variation dish was found. Not easy to find.) 10-3/8" W x 14-1/4" L, Mark: "Gonder Original," Script, Dijon. *Courtesy of Tom & Dixie Woodward.* Value: $100-125.

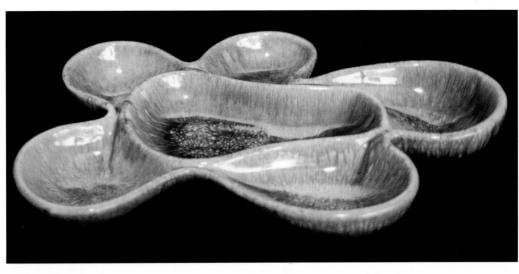

Chapter 8
Figurine Planters

This grouping causes more confusion with collectors than many others. Some of these pieces are very common, but sellers claim them to be rare. Harder to find than the individual pieces are complete sets, which are defined as the figurine accompanied by its planter. Another misconception concerns the Turbaned Woman Figurine with Basket Planter. Many people believe it to be a figurine candleholder when the basket planter is missing, leaving a slot at the top of her head that appears to fit a candle. While this figurine could be used for that, it is not the use Gonder intended. Also, where we believed only one size of this planter existed, two different sizes have now been found and identified. The Bali woman with no top is very elusive, since it was pulled from the market as too risqué for the time, and redesigned with a top and a different base. Finding one of the original figurines is considered a coup.

Mold #762, Turbaned Woman Figurine (Pair), with Basket Planters Missing (This figurine was only thought to be one size, but this now proves two different sizes were produced.), left: 11-1/2" H &, right: 13-1/4" H, Mark: "Gonder Ceramic Arts©," Block, left: Victorian Wine & right: Chartreuse. *Courtesy of Rod Emlet.* Value, with basket planter: $50-75; without basket planter: $10-20.

Mold #762, Turbaned Woman with Basket Planter Figurine. (This piece is sometimes misidentified as a candleholder, when the basket planter is missing; but, it is a figural planter. Hard to find with the basket planter.) 14-1/2" H x 5-3/4" W, Mark: "Gonder Ceramic Arts©," Block, Chartreuse. *Courtesy of Regina & Al Brown.* Value, with basket planter: $50-75; without basket planter: $10-20.

Mold #763, Bali Woman Figurine with No Top Planter Holder, on left. (This was the first Bali female figurine produced, but in 1950 it was considered to risqué to display nudity, so it was pulled and redesigned with a top. It is scarce. It is displayed here with a later figurine, with top, on right. Notice that the new figurine has a larger base and is taller and wider.) No top: 12-3/8" H x 9-1/8" W; with top: 13-1/8" H x 10-1/8" W; Mark on both: "©1950 Gonder Ceramic Arts," Block, Chartreuse. *Courtesy of Regina & Al Brown.* Value, no top, without gourds: $150-175.

Mold #763, Bali Woman Figurine with Top & Gourd Planters, front view (this piece is common), 13-1/8" H x 10-1/8" W, Mark: "©1950 Gonder Ceramic Arts," Block, Forest Green. Value with both Gourds: $45-65.

Mold #763, Bali Woman Figurine with Top & Gourd Planters, back view.

Mold #763, Bali Man Figurine with Gourd Planters, front view (this piece is common), 13-1/8" H x 10-1/2" W, Mark: "©1950 Gonder Ceramic Arts," Block, Forest Green. Value with both Gourds: $45-65.

Mold #764, Indian Figurine Porters Bearing Planter Bowl (very hard to find as a complete set), 12-1/4" H, Mark: "©1950 Gonder Ceramic Arts," Block, Victorian Wine. *Courtesy of Regina & Al Brown.* Value, complete with basket: $100-150.

Mold #763, Bali Man Figurine with Gourd Planters, back view.

Mold #765, Oriental Chair Bearer Figurine Planter Set (although the figurines appear often, the chair planter is scarce), 12" H, Mark: None, Chartreuse. *Courtesy of Regina & Al Brown.* Value, complete set: $150-175.

Mold #765, Oriental Chair Bearer Figurine Planter Holder, front view, 12" H, Mark: None, Chartreuse. *Courtesy of Regina & Al Brown.* Value, single: $40-50.

Mold #777, Oriental Water Bearer Woman Figurine Planter (this piece is very common), 14-1/4" H x 10-1/4" W, mark, stamp on bottom: "COPYWRITE GONDER CERAMIC ARTS," Block, Victorian Wine. Value, complete with bucket planters: $50-75.

Mold #766, Basque Dancers Figurine Planters Set (very hard to find), 12" H, Mark: None, Victorian Wine. *Courtesy of Bernice A. & Ralph H. Baker.* Value, complete set: $125-150.

Mold #777, Oriental Water Bearer Man Figurine Planter (this piece is very common), 14-1/8" H x 10-1/2" W, mark, stamp on bottom: "COPYWRITE GONDER CERAMIC ARTS," Block, Victorian Wine. Value, complete with bucket planters: $50-75.

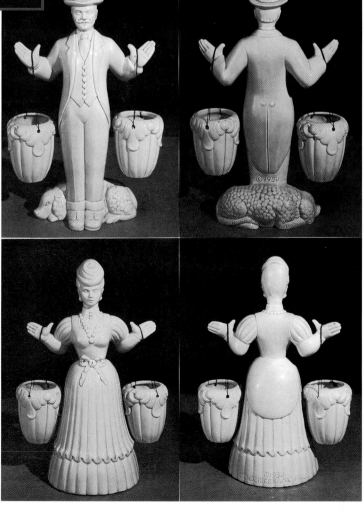

Mold #N/A, Gay '90s Man & Woman Figurine Planters (very hard to find), man: 13-1/4" H; woman: 14" H, Mark: "©1950 Gonder Ceramic Arts," Block, Catalog Sheets. Value for each, with buckets: $150-175.

Chapter 9
Figurines

Gonder loved figurines, both animals and those of his beloved Oriental lines. While the animal figurines are highly sought after by collectors, the Oriental figures can be more elusive. It takes a sharp eye to find these small Oriental figurines. During the photographing of this book, it was discovered that the panther figurines were produced in three lengths, with two of the lengths using the same mold number. You will need to carry a tape measure to know which is which. Several pieces in this grouping were developed as both figurines and lamp bases. They are included here rather than the lamp chapter, but are identified as possibilities for both groupings.

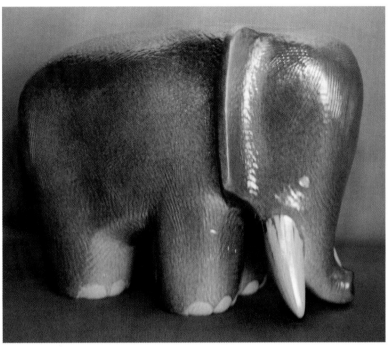

Mold #108, Large Elephant Figurine, stylized with ivory trim (scarce), 7-3/4" H x 10-1/4" L, Mark: "Gonder Original," Script, Onionskin. *Courtesy of Tom & Dixie Woodward.* Value: $400-500.

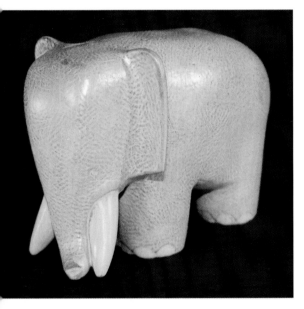

Mold #108, Elephant Figurine, stylized with ivory trim (scarce), different view and slightly different measurements, 7-1/2" H x 10" L, Mark: None, Onionskin. *Courtesy of Rod Emlet.* Value: $400-500.

Mold #205, Small Walking Panther Figurine, 3-1/8" H x 12-1/4" L, Mark: None, Red Flambé. *Courtesy of Regina & Al Brown.* Value, normally: $40-60, with this glaze: $60-90.

Mold #205, Medium Walking Panther Figurine. (Same mold number as previous small panther, but larger figure. Note tail difference from small figurine.) 3-1/4" H x 15-1/8" L, Mark: None, Turquoise Chinese Crackle. *Courtesy of Rod Emlet.* Value, normally: $60-80; with this glaze: $85-120.

Mold #206, Large Walking Panther Figurine (note that this panther has the left front foot forward, whereas the previous two have the right front foot forward), 4-1/8" H x 18-1/2" L, Mark: None, Red Flambé. *Courtesy of Regina & Al Brown.* Value, normally: $100-150; with this glaze: $150-180.

Mold #207, Large Elephant Figurine with raised trunk. (Determination that this is Gonder is usually made by looking at the ears when turned backwards. The ears are filled in or widened at the back. Also, the hole in the bottom is usually small. Since other pottery companies made this same type of figure, it is hard to determine Gonder without having a good background in glaze colors.) 8-7/8" H x 11-1/2" L, Mark: None, Gold Lustre. *Courtesy of Rod Emlet.* Value: $75 –100.

Mold #209, Small Elephant Figurine with Raised Trunk, 6-1/2" H x 8-1/4" L, Mark: None, Unusual Red-Orange. *Courtesy of Rod Emlet.* Value, normally: $40-50; with this red-orange glaze: $70-80.

Mold #210, Large Reclining Panther Figurine, 6-1/2" H x 18-1/2" L, Mark: "Gonder Original 210," Script, Royal Purple. *Courtesy of Rod Emlet.* Value, normally: $100-150; with this unusual glaze: $200-250.

Mold #212, Rooster Figurine (hard to find), 10-1/2" H x 4" W, Mark: None, Rutile Green. *Courtesy of Rod Emlet.* Value: $150-175.

Mold #209, Small Elephant Figurine with Raised Trunk (reverse view). *Courtesy of Rod Emlet.*

Mold #213, Doe with Turned Head Figurine, 10-5/8" H x 3" W x 4-1/2" L, Mark: None, Green with Sponged White. *Courtesy of Rod Emlet.* Value: $40-50.

Mold #213 & #218, Doe with Turned Head Figurine & Side
Planters; Doe: 10-5/8" H x 3" W x 4-1/2" L; Planters: 2-3/4" H x
3-3/4" W x 3" L, Mark: None, Dijon. *Courtesy of Rod Emlet.*
Value, with planters: $75-100.

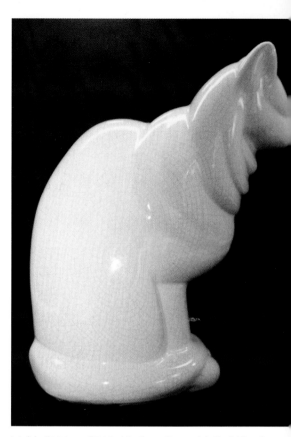

Mold #521 or #208, Modern "Imperial Cat" Figurine
(this figurine has been found in two different heights,
this being the smaller), 12-1/4" H, Mark: "Gonder
USA," Script, Chinese White Crackle. *Courtesy of Rod
Emlet.* Value, normally: $225-275; with this glaze:
$290-355.

Mold #217, Small Reclining Panther Figurine, 5-1/2" H x 14-3/4" L, Mark:
"Gonder Original 217," Script, Red Flambé. *Courtesy of Rod Emlet.* Value,
normally: $75-95; with this glaze: $110-140.

Mold #521, Modern "Imperial Cat" Figurine,
12-1/8" H x 5-3/4" W, Mark: "Gonder USA
521," Script, Gunmetal Black. Value: $200-250.

Mold #525, Gamecock with Flowers Figurine Pair. (Note: there are distinct differences in the tail feathers and wings of the two figures. The left one has plain tail feathers and a distinct wing; the other doesn't. Not easy to find.) 10-3/4" H x 7-1/8" W, Mark: None, left: Dijon, right: Sea Swirl. Value: $150-175.

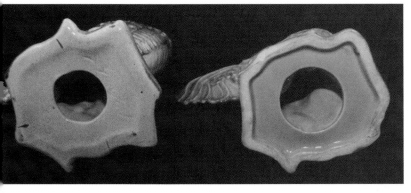

Mold #525, Hen with Worm Figurine (not easy to find), 6-3/4" H x 9" L, Mark: None, Dijon. *Courtesy of Rod Emlet.* Value: $125-150.

Mold #541, Oriental Chinese Coolie Head Figurine. (These pieces have also been seen as lamp bases. Scarce.) 10-3/4" H, Mark: "Gonder 541 USA," Script, Gold Lustre. *Courtesy of Rod Emlet.* Value, normally: $400-500; with this glaze: $500-600.

Left: Mold #525, Gamecock with Flowers Figurine Pair Bottoms. (Bottoms of previous two figures. Note the left bottom that displays the three straight line stilt marks from the firing blocks.)

Below: Mold #541, Oriental Chinese Coolie Head Figurine (another view in a different glaze), 11" H x 11-1/2" W, Mark: None, Chinese White Crackle. *Courtesy of Regina & Al Brown.* Value, normally: $400-500; with this glaze: $550-650.

Mold #545, Oriental Standing Coolie Figurine, 8-1/8" H, Mark: "Gonder U.S.A.," Script, Custom Paint. *Courtesy of Tom & Dixie Woodward.* Value, normally: $15-30; with this glaze: $50-75.

Mold #547, Oriental Figurine Kneeling, 6" H, Mark: "Gonder 547," Script, Antique Gold Crackle. *Courtesy of Rod Emlet.* Value, normally: $15-30; with this glaze: $25-50.

Mold #549, Madonna Figurine Standing (very hard to find), 9-1/4" H, Mark: "Gonder 549 U.S.A.," Script, Antique Gold Crackle. *Courtesy of Regina & Al Brown.* Value, normally: $50-75; with this glaze: $85-125.

Mold #545, Oriental Standing Coolie Figurine (Pair), 7-3/4" H, mark, both: "Gonder USA," Script, left: Charcoal, right: Burgundy. *Courtesy of Rod Emlet.* Value, normally: $15-30; with these glazes: $30-50.

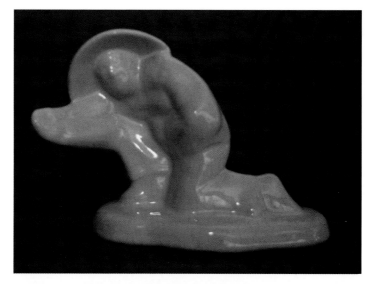

Mold #546, Oriental Figurine, Reaching, 4-5/8" H x 6-1/2" W, Mark: None, Mother Of Pearl. *Courtesy of Tom & Dixie Woodward.* Value: $25-40.

Mold #551, Oriental Man Figurines (Pair), 7-1/4"
H, Mark: "Gonder 551 U.S.A.," Block, left:
Chartreuse, & right: French Lilac. *Courtesy of Regina
& Al Brown.* Value, each: $40-60.

Mold #570, Oriental
Woman Figurine Hands
Together, 6-1/4'H, Mark:
None, Rutile Green. *Courtesy
of Tom & Dixie Woodward.*
Value: $40-60.

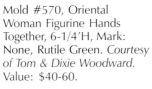

Mold #573, Oriental Woman
Figurine Holding Ginger Jar,
4-7/8" H, Mark: None,
Chartreuse. *Courtesy of Tom
& Dixie Woodward.* Value:
$40-60.

Mold #581, Jester Head Figurine or Lamp Base,
front view. (Only two of these figures have surfaced
to date, but we are sure there are more out there.
Rare.) 13-3/4" H, marked on front: "Cogito Ergo
Sum," no other mark, Gunmetal Black. *Courtesy of
Rod Emlet.* Value: $400-500.

Mold #581, Jester Head Figurine or Lamp Base,
side view. *Courtesy of Rod Emlet.*

Mold #587, Young Woman Figurine or Lamp, 9-3/16" H x 4-1/4" W x 4-1/4" L, Mark: None, Chartreuse. Value: $125-150.

Mold #690, Two Running Deer Figurine (hard to find), 6" H x 9-1/4" L, Mark: "Gonder Original 690," Script, Rutile Green. *Courtesy of Rod Emlet.* Value: $75-100.

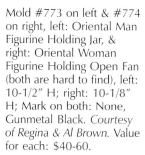

Mold #772, Fatima Figurine, Pair (hard to find), 9-1/2" H, mark, on front: "MARIAE VIRGINIS DE FATIMA," Block, White with Gold Trim. *Courtesy of Tom & Dixie Woodward.* Value with Original Rosary: $75-100; without Rosary: $40-60.

Mold #773 on left & #774 on right, left: Oriental Man Figurine Holding Jar, & right: Oriental Woman Figurine Holding Open Fan (both are hard to find), left: 10-1/2" H; right: 10-1/8" H; Mark on both: None, Gunmetal Black. *Courtesy of Regina & Al Brown.* Value for each: $40-60.

Mold #588, Rose Lady Head Figurine or Lamp, 12-1/4" H, Mark: None, Blue. *Courtesy of Regina & Al Brown.* Value: $150-175.

Mold #775, Oriental Bearded Man Figurine (hard to find), 8-5/8" H, Mark: None, Victorian Wine. *Courtesy of Tom & Dixie Woodward.* Value, in mint condition: $50-60; with this chip: $40-50.

Mold #872, Horse Head Figurine, Racing. (This figurine was previously known in only one size and mold number. Hard to find.) 7" H x 15" L, Mark: "Gonder Original 872," Script, Rutile Green. *Courtesy of Rod Emlet.* Value: $150-175.

Mold #776, Oriental Woman Figurine with Right Hand to Head & Left Hand Holding Fan (hard to find), 9" H, Mark: None, Rutile Green. *Courtesy of Tom & Dixie Woodward.* Value: $60-80.

Mold # 874, Horse Head Figurine, Racing (hard to find), 5-3/4" H x 13-1/2" L, Mark: "Gonder Original 874," Script, Red Flambé. *Courtesy of Bernice A. & Ralph H. Baker.* Value, normally: $150-175; with this glaze: $225-260.

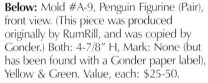

Below: Mold #A-9, Penguin Figurine (Pair), front view. (This piece was produced originally by RumRill, and was copied by Gonder.) Both: 4-7/8" H, Mark: None (but has been found with a Gonder paper label), Yellow & Green. Value, each: $25-50.

Mold #A9, Penguin Figurine (Pair), side views.

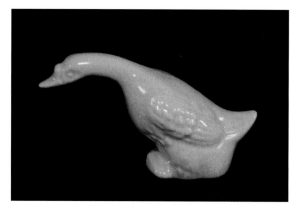

Mold #B-14, Low Goose Figurine, 3-1/8" H x 5-3/4" L, Mark: None, Coral Lustre. *Courtesy of Rod Emlet.* Value: $25-40.

Mold #B-15, High Goose Figurine, 5-1/2" H, Mark: None, Coral Lustre. *Courtesy of Rod Emlet.* Value: $25-40.

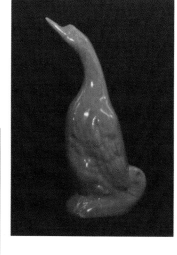

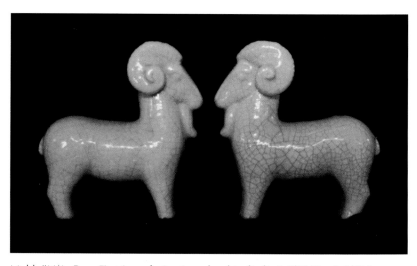

Mold #N/A, Oriental Man Figurine with Right Hand Up (hard to find), 6-3/4" H, Mark: None, Pistachio. *Courtesy of Tom & Dixie Woodward.* Value: $40-60.

Mold #N/A, Oriental Figurine or Lamp Base, Man and Woman, Pair (hard to find), 16-3/4" H, Mark: None, Turquoise. *Courtesy of Rod Emlet.* Value for pair: $175-200.

Mold #N/A, Ram Figurines, facing (very hard to find), 6-1/8" H x 5-3/4" L, Mark: None, Chinese White Crackle. *Courtesy of Ron & Alma Hoopes.* Value, each, normally: $75-100; with this glaze: $95-130.

Mold #N/A, St. Francis Figurine Base, displaying the mark discussed.

Mold #N/A, St. Francis Figurine. (This figurine was originally made for the bird bath set; see catalog pages. Rare.) 17-1/2" H, Mark: "1954 Lawton Gonder" (this is the only piece of Gonder found marked in this fashion), Block, Multi-colored. *Courtesy of Regina & Al Brown.* Value: $400-500.

An early advertisement from Gonder showing the St. Francis Figurine as a set with the Gonder Bird Bath and stand. All of these are considered rare.

Chapter 10
Flower Frogs & Cigarette Holders

Only one separate flower frog has been found to date, but others probably exist. They were a popular addition to many console bowls. The cigarette holders line was developed as the Sovereign line, in most cases. The "Sovereign" line was a name given to a group of fluted pieces. It signified an elegant design. All Sovereign pieces were marked with a paper label only. They usually were not impressed with a Gonder marking, but had a paper label attached signifying the line name. Since these labels may have been removed, a collector must know the line's characteristics and styles to be able to identify pieces from this line.

Mold #N/A, Flower Frog, 3-5/8" W, Mark: None, Nubian Black. *Courtesy of Tom & Dixie Woodward.* Value: $20-30.

Mold #250, 3-Tier Flower Frog with Original Box, 2-5/8" H x 5-7/8" W, Mark: "PATENT # 2496758," Block, Forest Green. Value, with original box: $100-125; without box: $75-100.

Mold #801, Sovereign Cigarette Holder, Urn Shaped & Footed, 3-1/2" H, Mark: Paper Label, "Sovereign Gonder U.S.A.," White. *Courtesy of Regina & Al Brown.* Value: $40-60.

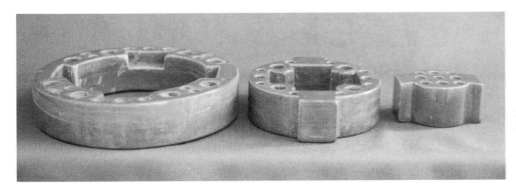

Mold #250, 3-Tier Flower Frog, separated.

Mold #802, Sovereign Fluted Cigarette Holder, 3-5/8" H, Mark: "Sovereign Gonder U.S.A.," Block, White. *Courtesy of Regina & Al Brown.* Value: $40-60.

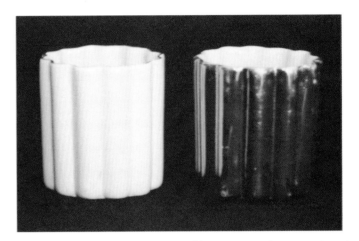

Mold #804, Sovereign Cigarette Holders (Pair), 2-5/8" H, Mark: None, Chinese White Crackle & Antique Gold Crackle. *Courtesy of Tom & Dixie Woodward.* Value, White Crackle: $50-75; Antique Gold Crackle: $70-100.

Mold #804, Sovereign Fluted Cigarette Holder, 2-5/8" H, Mark: "Sovereign Gonder U.S.A.," Block, White. *Courtesy of Regina & Al Brown.* Value: $40-60.

Mold #806, Sovereign Cigarette Box, 2-5/8" H x 3-1/2" W x 4-3/8" L, Mark: None, White. *Courtesy of Regina & Al Brown.* Value: $60-80.

Chapter 11
Jars

Oriental ginger jars were a Gonder favorite, as was anything Oriental. Most of this line also included a base for the ginger jar to rest upon, and all had lids, which you may or may not find with them today. This line included much use of Gonder's crackle glazes, and most pieces are found in these colors.

Mold #533, Oriental Ginger Jar with Lid, Dragon Motif, 7-3/4" H, Mark: "Gonder 533," Script, Turquoise Chinese Crackle. *Courtesy of Regina & Al Brown.* Value, normally: $75-100; with this glaze: $ 105-140.

Mold #529, Oriental Plum Jar with Lid (very hard to find), 9-3/16" H, Mark: "Gonder 529," Script, Chinese White Crackle. Value with Lid: $125-150.

Mold #530 & #530B, Square Ginger Jar with Lid & Base, Jar: 10-1/2" H, Mark on jar: "Gonder 530 U.S.A.;" Mark on base: unreadable (but known to be #530B), Script, Antique Gold Crackle. *Courtesy of Ron & Alma Hoopes.* Value, complete, usually: $100-150; in this glaze: $170-255. Value, base alone: $40-60.

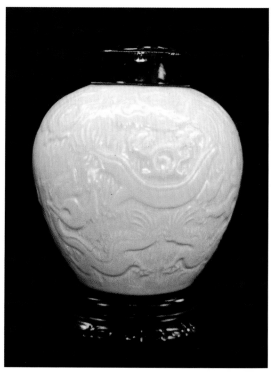

Mold #533 & #533B, Oriental Ginger Jar with Lid & Base (complete set is very hard to find), Dragon Motif, 7-3/4" H, Jar Mark: "Gonder USA 533;" Base Mark: "Gonder 533B," Script, Jar: Ming Yellow; Base & Lid: Nubian Black. *Courtesy of Rod Emlet.* Value with Base: $150-175.

Chapter 12
La Gonda

La Gonda was a dinnerware line produced in the late 1940s and early 1950s to compete with popular dinnerware such as Homer Laughlin's Fiesta and Riviera lines. People liked the colorful glazes and square shapes. The line was not produced for long. Customers found that the pieces chipped easily, and sales dropped. A complete set of La Gonda in excellent condition today will bring a premium price.

Mold #905, La Gonda Fruit Bowl, 4-3/8" W x 4-3/8" L, Mark: "This piece individually handcrafted by Gonder," Script, Turquoise Green. *Courtesy of Tom & Dixie Woodward.* Value: $15-20.

Mold #396, La Gonda Rectangular Teapot, 6-1/4" H, Mark: "396," Block, Forest Green with White Sponge. *Courtesy of Bernice A. & Ralph H. Baker.* Value: $50-75.

Mold #903 (Tea Cup) & #904 (Saucer), La Gonda Square Tea Cup & Saucer Set, Tea Cup: 2-1/2" W x 3-1/4" L; Saucer: 5-3/8" W x 5-3/8" L, Mark, both: "This piece individually handcrafted by Gonder," Script, Coral. *Courtesy of Tom & Dixie Woodward.* Value, Tea Cup: $8-10; Saucer: $8-10.

Mold #907, La Gonda Cream Pitcher, 4" H x 7" W, Mark: None, Yellow. *Courtesy of Tom & Dixie Woodward.* Value: $15-20.

Mold #908, La Gonda Double Handled Cream Soup Bowl with Lid, 3-3/8" H x 4-1/2" W x 5-3/4" L, Mark: "908," Block, Rutile Green with White Sponge. *Courtesy of Regina & Al Brown.* Value: $20-25.

Mold #912, La Gonda Oblong Chop Plate, top view. (Scarce. Very hard to find in mint condition.) 8-7/8" W x 12-1/4" L, Mark: "This piece individually handcrafted by Gonder," Script, Pistachio. *Courtesy of Bernice A. & Ralph H. Baker.* Value: $100-125.

Mold #913, La Gonda S&P Shakers, 3" H, Mark: None, Turquoise Green & Yellow. *Courtesy of Tom & Dixie Woodward.* Value: $15-20.

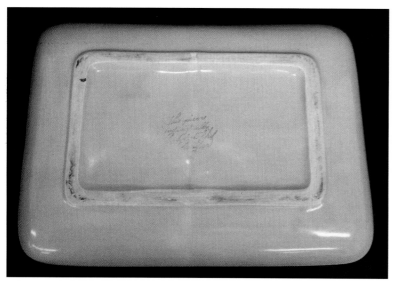

Mold #912, La Gonda Oblong Chop Plate, bottom view. *Courtesy of Bernice A. & Ralph H. Baker.*

Mold #914, La Gonda Teapot, 7" H x 8-1/4" W, Mark: "This piece individually handcrafted by Gonder," Script, Yellow. *Courtesy of Tom & Dixie Woodward.* Value: $50-75.

Mold #915, La Gonda Candleholders, 2-1/8" H x 2" W x 2" L, Mark: None, Yellow. *Courtesy of Tom & Dixie Woodward.* Value: $15-20.

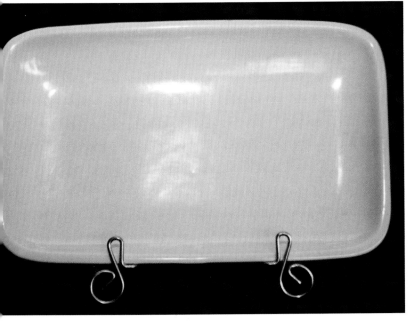

Mold #916, La Gonda Server Bowl, 5-7/8" W x 9-5/8" L, Mark: "This piece individually handcrafted by Gonder," Script, Yellow. *Courtesy of Tom & Dixie Woodward.* Value: $20-30.

Mold #917, La Gonda Pitcher, 8-1/8" H x 9" W, Mark: "Gonder Original 917," Script, Victorian Wine with Volcanic White Drip. *Courtesy of Rod Emlet.* Value: $40-50.

Mold #916 (Plate) & #909 (Mug), La Gonda Snack Set, Oblong Platter & 17 oz. Mug (as a set, not easy to find), Mug: 4-7/8" H; platter: 5-3/4" W x 9-1/2" L; Mark: "This piece individually handcrafted by Gonder," Script, Turquoise Green. *Courtesy of Tom & Dixie Woodward.* Value, as set: $40-50.

Mold #917 & #909, La Gonda Pitcher & Mug Set, Pitcher: 8-1/8" H x 9" W, Pitcher Mark: "Gonder Original 917," Script, White with Dark Blue Swirl Lines. (Lawton Gonder's daughter, Mrs. Kay Nagi, reports that this glaze was only used on a set like this twice.) *Courtesy of P.J. Watson.* Value: $125-150.

Mold #923, La Gonda Creamer & Sugar Stack Set, 2-7/8" H x 3-7/8" W x 4" L, Mark: "Gonder Original 923," Script, Forest Green with White Volcanic Drip. *Courtesy of Rod Emlet.* Value: $30-40.

Mold #952, La Gonda Small Covered Custard with Handle, 3-1/4" H, Mark: "Gonder Original 952," Script, Black Top & White Base. *Courtesy of Rod Emlet.* Value: $15-25.

Mold #952, La Gonda Small Covered Custard with Handle, 3-1/4" H, Mark: "Gonder Original 952," Script, White with Maroon Sponge. *Courtesy of Rod Emlet.* Value: $15-25.

Mold #952, La Gonda 1-pint Small Covered Custards with Handle, bottom view, 3-3/8" H x 4-1/2" W x 6-1/2" L, Mark: "Gonder 952 Original," Script, Sponged Green with White Volcanic Drip. Value: $15-25.

Mold #953, La Gonda Medium Covered Bowl with Handle, 4" H x 8-1/4" W x 5-1/4" L, "Gonder Original 953," Script, Forest Green with White Volcanic Sponge. *Courtesy of Rod Emlet.* Value: $20-30.

Mold #954, La Gonda Large Covered Casserole Bowl with Handle (side view), 5-1/4" H x 6-1/2" W x 10-1/8" L, Mark: "Gonder Original 954," Script, Victorian Wine with Volcanic White Drip. Value: $30-40.

Mold #954, La Gonda Large Covered Casserole Bowl with Handle (bottom view).

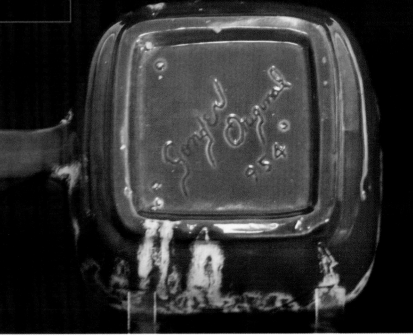

Mold #955, La Gonda Double Handle Casserole Bowl with Tab Handle Lid (hard to find), 5-3/8" H x 6-3/4" W x 11" L, Mark: "Gonder Original 955," Script, White with Brown Sponge. *Courtesy of Rod Emlet.* Value: $75-100.

Mold #Misc., La Gonda Dinnerware Set. Displayed as an almost complete set for eight at a Gonder Reunion Meeting, July 1998. Most pieces marked: "This piece individually handcrafted by Gonder," Script. *Courtesy of Rod Emlet.* Value of displayed set: $400-500.

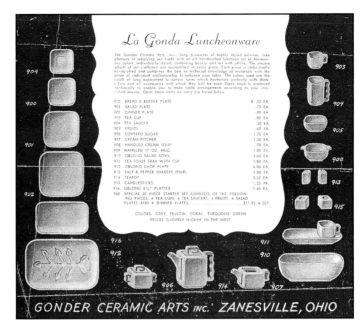

A La Gonda Luncheon Ware advertising sheet sent to clients, displaying both prices and designs of each piece.

A window display of La Gonda dinnerware, in the Sunshine Yellow glaze, so states the sign at the bottom. We wonder what the sale prices were then?

Chapter 13
Lamps

This is one of the hardest lines to identify as produced by Gonder. Through his lamp producing company, Elgee Pottery, Gonder made many lamps, but did not mark them as Elgee or Gonder. Most were made under contract for the Bradley Manufacturing Company, Chicago, Illinois, and were sold with their paper labels attached. Without the catalog sales pages we have been able to acquire, it would have been impossible to identify many of these lamps. A good knowledge of Gonder's glazes also helps with identification, but many lamps were produced in non-Gonder traditional glaze treatments. Most lamps were manufactured from a very white clay and display glaze dripping into the interior. The interiors were usually never fully glazed. We have included several more lamps in chapter 22 (Possible Gonder) at the end of the book.

Mold #522, Scarla Sunfish Lamp (also made as a vase), 9" H x 11" L, Mark: None, Sea Swirl. *Courtesy of Bernice A. & Ralph H. Baker.* Value: $100-125.

Mold #207, Large Elephant Lamp Base (very hard to find), 9-1/4" H x 10-3/4" L, Mark: None, Forest Green. *Courtesy of Regina & Al Brown.* Value: $125-150.

Catalog #1226, Driftwood Lamps (Pair), 11-1/2" H, Mark: None, left: Cocoa & right: Wheat. *Courtesy of Rod Emlet.* Value, each: $60-80.

Catalog #1901, Horse Head Television or Console Lamp, 14-3/8" H, Mark: None, Forest Green. *Courtesy of Regina & Al Brown.* Value: $75-100.

Catalog #1903, Schooner TV Lamp, 13" H, Mark: None, Cocoa with White Drip. *Courtesy of Tom & Dixie Woodward.* Valu Value: $50-75.

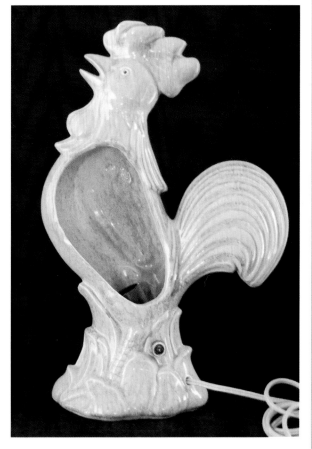

Catalog #1902, Chanticleer TV Lamp (front view), 14-1/4" H x 9-1/2" W, Mark: None, Pistachio. Value: $100-125.

Catalog #1902, Chanticleer TV Lamp (back view).

Catalog #1905, Mill TV Lamp (very hard to find), 8-1/2" H x 12" W, Mark: None, Brown with Green Accent. *Courtesy of Bernice A. & Ralph H. Baker.* Value: $75-100.

Catalog #2020, Double Swirl Lamp, 30" H, Mark: None, Cocoa. *Courtesy of Diana L. Hansen.* Value: $40-60.

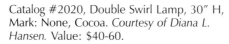

Right: Catalog #2067, Frappe Lamp. (Provenance on this particular lamp has it being used by Lawton Gonder's secretary on her desk.) 15-3/4" H, Mark: None, Rutile Green with Green Overlay. *Courtesy of Rod Emlet.* Value, normally: $50-75, but with this provenance: $75-100.

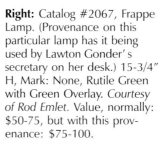

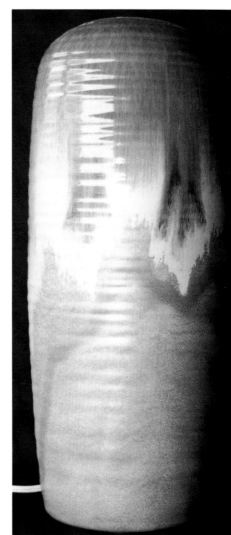

Catalog #2017, Driftwood Lamp, 30" H, Mark: None, Pistachio. *Courtesy of Diana L. Hansen.* Value: $75-100.

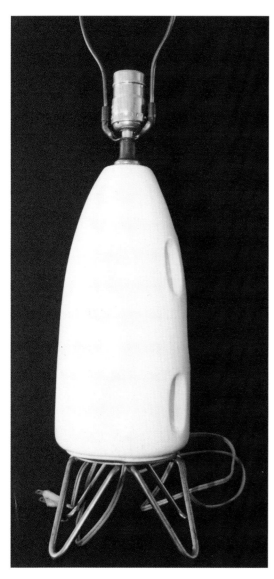

Catalog #2228, Bullet Lamp (back bottom view).
Courtesy of Regina & Al Brown.

Catalog #2228, Bullet Lamp (front view), 11" H,
Mark: None, but displays "Genuine Kingsbridge
Lamp" Paper Label on back (see back bottom
view), White. *Courtesy of Regina & Al Brown.* Value:
$75-100.

Catalog #2255, Scroll Lamp, 12-3/4" H,
Mark: None, Forest Green. *Courtesy of
Bernice A. & Ralph H. Baker.* Value: $75-100.

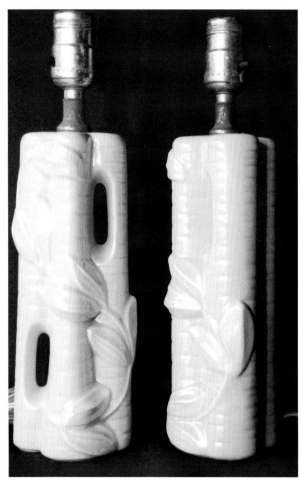

Catalog #4037, Geometric Planes Lamp, 10" H x 9" W,
Mark: None, Dijon. *Courtesy of Bernice A. & Ralph H. Baker.*
Value: $40-60.

Catalog #3031, Vine & Leaves Lamp (Pair), 9-1/2" H,
Mark: None, Pistachio. *Courtesy of Rod Emlet.* Value,
each: $40-60.

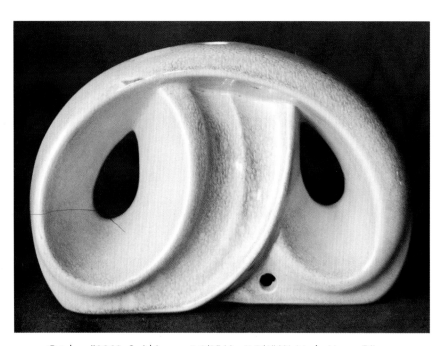

Catalog #3060, Swirl Lamp, 5-1/2" H x 7-3/4" W, Mark: None, Dijon.
Courtesy of Rod Emlet. Value: $40-60.

Catalog #4039, Double Link Lamp (Pair), 24-1/2" H,
Mark: None, left: Chartreuse & right: Black. *Courtesy
of Diana L. Hansen.* Value: $45-65.

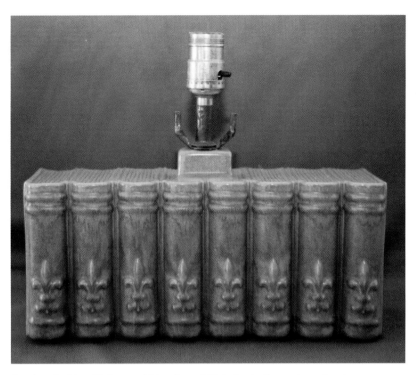

Catalog #5087, Hollywood Headboard Unit Books Lamp (very hard to find), 6-3/8" H x 11-1/2" W, Mark: None, Rutile Green. *Courtesy of Regina & Al Brown.* Value: $125-150.

Catalog #4046, Ewer Lamp, 11" H, Mark: None, Italian Pink Crackle. Value, normally: $35-55; with this glaze: $55-75.

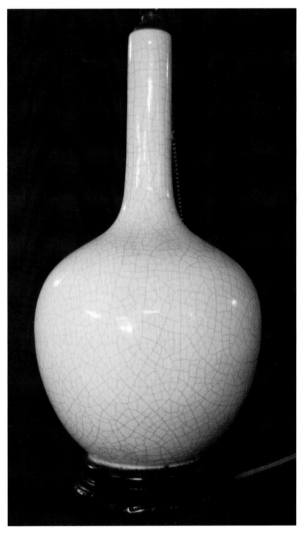

Catalog #4085, Keystone Lamp, 10" H x 9-1/2" W, Mark: None, Dijon. *Courtesy of Rod Emlet.* Value: $40-60.

Catalog #5506, Tall Bottle Lamp (very hard to find), 17-1/2" H, Mark: None, Ivory Crackle. *Courtesy of Ron & Alma Hoopes.* Value: $100-125.

Catalog #5507, Dogwood Globe Lamp (scarce), 15-1/4" H, Mark: None, Italian Pink Crackle. *Courtesy of Ron & Alma Hoopes*. Value, normally: $175-200; with this glaze: $200-250.

Mold #H-77, Double Handle with Vine Leaves Lamp with Metal Base, 10-1/4" H, Mark: None, Ming Yellow. *Courtesy of Rod Emlet*. Value: $50-75.

Catalog #N/A, Double Inverted "G" Lamp, 6-3/4" H x 11-1/2" W, Mark: None, Dijon. *Courtesy of Rod Emlet*. Value: $40-60.

Catalog #N/A, Bonsai Tree Lamp with Ridged Sides (hard to find), 11-3/8" H x 4-3/4" W x 10-1/8" L, Mark: "24," Chartreuse. Value: $175-200.

Catalog #N/A, Cactus Lamp, 15-1/2" H, Mark: None, Pistachio. *Courtesy of Rod Emlet.* Value: $75-100.

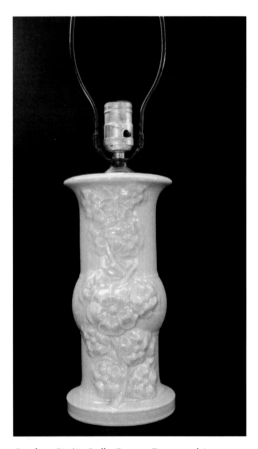

Catalog #N/A, Bulb Center Dogwood Lamp, 10-3/4" H, Mark: None, Pink. *Courtesy of Rod Emlet.* Value: $50-70.

Catalog #N/A, Kneeling Coolie Lamp (Pair), 11-1/4" H, Mark: None, Ivory Crackle. *Courtesy of Rod Emlet*. Value: $75-100.

Catalog #N/A, Chinese Foo Dog Lamp Base, front view (very hard to find), 7-3/4" H x 7" L, Mark: None, Rutile Green. *Courtesy of Regina & Al Brown*. Value: $125-150.

Catalog #N/A, Chinese Foo Dog Lamp Base, back view (very hard to find). *Courtesy of Regina & Al Brown*.

Catalog #N/A, Figure Eight Swirl Lamp, 15-5/8" H, Mark: None, Black. *Courtesy of Rod Emlet*. Value: $75-100.

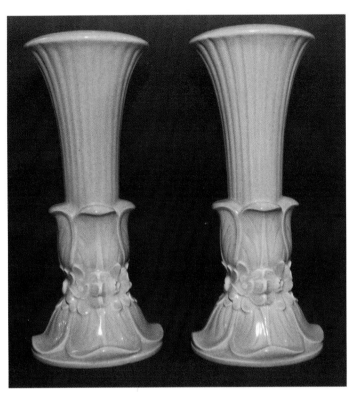

Catalog #N/A, Flower & Leaves Lamp, 11-1/2" H, Mark: None, Dove Gray. *Courtesy of Rod Emlet.* Value, each: $40-60.

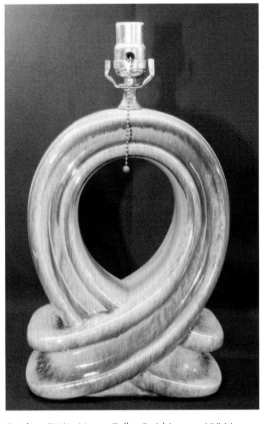

Catalog #N/A, Horse Collar Swirl Lamp, 10" H x 9-1/4" W, Mark: None, Wine Brown. *Courtesy of Rod Emlet.* Value: $40-60.

Catalog #N/A, Globe Lamp, 10-3/4" H, Mark: None, Royal Blue with Volcanic White Drip. *Courtesy of Rod Emlet.* Value: $40-60.

Catalog #N/A, Rearing Horse with Leaves Lamp, 12-3/4" H, Mark: None, Pistachio. *Courtesy of Regina & Al Brown.* Value: $75-100.

Catalog #N/A, Rearing Horse Lamp, 14-1/4" H, Mark: None, Dijon. *Courtesy of Rod Emlet.* Value: $75-100.

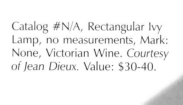

Catalog #N/A, Rectangular Ivy Lamp, no measurements, Mark: None, Victorian Wine. *Courtesy of Jean Dieux.* Value: $30-40.

Catalog #N/A, Rearing Horse Lamp with Planters, 12-1/2" H x 4" W, Mark: None, Black. *Courtesy of Bernice A. & Ralph H. Baker.* Value, with planters: $125-150; without planters: $100-125.

Catalog #N/A, " LG" Lamp. (So named because if you turn the lamp upside down, you will see it is the initials " L" & "G," for Lawton Gonder.) 8-1/2" H x 6-3/8" W, Mark: None, Gunmetal Black. Value: $75-100.

Catalog #N/A, Lyre Lamp, 15" H, Mark: None, Wine Brown. *Courtesy of Ron & Alma Hoopes.* Value: $75-100.

Catalog #N/A, Magnolias with Leaves Lamp, 10" H, Mark: None, Pistachio. *Courtesy of Rod Emlet.* Value: $40-60.

Catalog #N/A, Magnolia Lamp, 10-7/8" H x 5-1/4" W, Mark: None, White with Shell Pink Flowers. *Courtesy of Rod Emlet.* Value: $40-50.

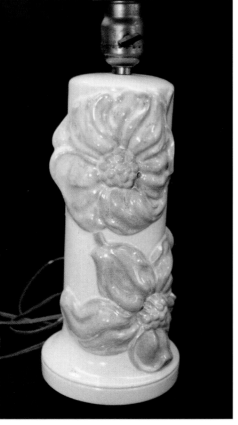

Catalog #N/A, Raised Nude Woman Lamp, 9-1/2" H, Mark: None, Chartreuse. *Courtesy of Rod Emlet.* Value: $100-125.

Catalog #N/A, Oriental Figures with Post Lamp (very hard to find), 16" H, Mark: None, Pistachio. *Courtesy of Rod Emlet.* Value: $200-250.

Catalog #N/A, Oriental Woman Lamp, 18-5/8" H x 9-7/8" W, Mark: None, Chinese White Crackle. *Courtesy of Rod Emlet.* Value: $200-250.

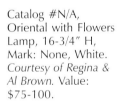

Catalog #N/A, Oriental with Flowers Lamp, 16-3/4" H, Mark: None, White. *Courtesy of Regina & Al Brown.* Value: $75-100.

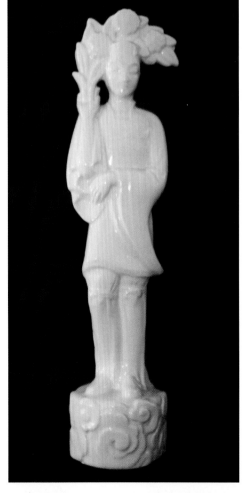

Catalog #N/A, Pagoda with Coolie Lamp, 13-1/4" H x 11-1/4" L, Mark: None, Chartreuse. *Courtesy of Ron & Alma Hoopes.* Value: $125-150.

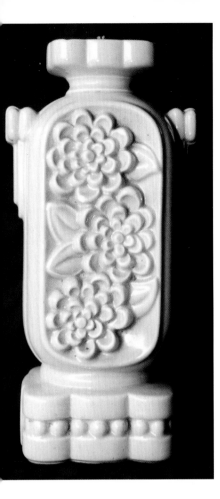

Right: Catalog #N/A, Rectangular Flower Center Lamp, 11" H x 4-1/8" W x 6-1/8" L, Mark: None, Cocoa. *Courtesy of Bernice A. & Ralph H. Baker.* Value: $25-40.

Left: Catalog #N/A, Pedestal with Chrysanthemums Lamp, 12-1/4" H, Mark: None, Pistachio. *Courtesy of Rod Emlet.* Value: $40-60.

Catalog #N/A, Picture Frame Tube Lamp, 11" H, Mark: None, but a paper label "Genuine Kingsbridge Lamp" & a "Kingsbridge" tag, Wine Brown. *Courtesy of Regina & Al Brown.* Value: $50-75.

Catalog #N/A, Reverse Swans Lamp, 10-1/4" H, Mark: None, Pale Blue Crackle. *Courtesy of Rod Emlet.* Value: $50-75.

Catalog #N/A, Small Rocket Lamp, 7-3/4" H,
Mark: None, Gold Lustre with Black Swirl. *Courtesy
of Rod Emlet.* Value: $125-150.

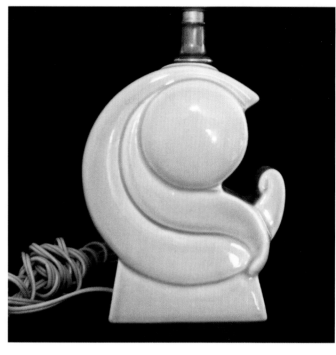

Catalog #N/A, Swirled G Shape Lamp, 6-1/16" H x 3-1/2" W x
4-3/4" L, Mark: None, Gray. Value: $25-35.

Catalog #N/A, Square Footed Lamp, 9-3/8" H,
Mark: None, Dove Gray with White Volcanic Drip.
Courtesy of Rod Emlet. Value: $35-50.

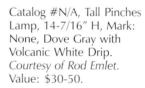

Catalog #N/A, Tall Pinches
Lamp, 14-7/16" H, Mark:
None, Dove Gray with
Volcanic White Drip.
Courtesy of Rod Emlet.
Value: $30-50.

Chapter 14
Lazy Susans

We have separated these three to show a previously unknown fact. Gonder produced three totally different sizes of Lazy Susans, with the largest also including double salt and pepper shakers. If you have one of these sets, now you must search for the other two to complete the collection. Good luck! They are not easy to find.

Mold #8, Small Lazy Susan (hard to find), 9-1/2" W, Mark: " LG," Script, Turquoise & Black. *Courtesy of Rod Emlet.* Value: $N/P.

Mold #8, Medium Lazy Susan (hard to find), 11-1/2" W, Mark: " LG," Script, Brown & Yellow. *Courtesy of Rod Emlet.* Value: $N/P.

Mold #8, Large Lazy Susan with Salt & Pepper Shakers (very hard to find), 17" W, Mark: None, White with Wine Drip. *Courtesy of Tom & Dixie Woodward.* Value: $N/P.

Chapter 15
Mugs & Pitchers

The only mug shown here is the twisted handle mug. Most other mugs are shown within the lines they are identified with, such as La Gonda. We have also found a mug previously unknown to us, and it is shown in the ashtray chapter, where it is part of a set that included an ashtray base. Gonder made many pitchers, including the elusive lizard handle pitcher (Mold #J-54), which collector's will want to add to their collections.

Mold #902, Twisted Handle Mug, 5-1/4" H x 3-7/8" W, Mark: "Gonder 902," Script, Rutile Green with Raised ridged lines. *Courtesy of Rod Emlet.* Value: $15-30.

Mold #104, Full Upper Handle & Lower Knob Pitcher, right view. (Rare. Only 2-3 of these have been found to date.) 12-1/2" H, Mark: "Gonder Original," Script, Onionskin. *Courtesy of Tom & Dixie Woodward.* Value: $N/P

Mold #104, Full Upper Handle & Lower Knob Pitcher, left view. *Courtesy of Tom & Dixie Woodward.* Value: $N/P.

Mold #102 & # N/A, Pistol Grip Pitcher & Mug (very hard to find), 9-1/8" H, Mark: "Gonder Original," Script, Onionskin. *Courtesy of Tom & Dixie Woodward.* Value, Pitcher: $125-150; Mug: $30-50.

Mold #301, Twisted Handle Twig Pitcher, right view (hard to find), 7-7/8" H x 7-1/2" L, Mark: "Gonder 301," Script, Wheat with Cocoa. *Courtesy of Rod Emlet.* Value: $100-125.

Mold #606 or #H-606, Classical Pitcher, 9-1/4" H, Mark: "606 Gonder USA," Script, Coral Lustre. *Courtesy of Rod Emlet.* Value: $75-100.

Mold #301, Twisted Handle Twig Pitcher, left view. *Courtesy of Rod Emlet.*

Mold #682, Two Bands Pitcher, 10" H, Mark: "Gonder Original 682," Script, Dijon. *Courtesy of Regina & Al Brown.* Value: $50-75.

Mold #901, Squashed Twig Pitcher, 8-5/16" H x 7-3/4" L, Mark: "Gonder Original 901," Script, Dijon. *Courtesy of Regina & Al Brown.* Value: $50-75.

Mold #1206, Ruffled Lip Pitcher, 6-3/4" H, Mark: "Gonder Original 1206," Script, Dijon. *Courtesy of Bernice A. & Ralph H. Baker.* Value: $40-60.

Mold #1205, Question Mark Handle Pitcher, 8-1/2" H, Mark: "1205 Gonder Original," Script, Forest Green. *Courtesy of Bernice A. & Ralph H. Baker.* Value: $50-75.

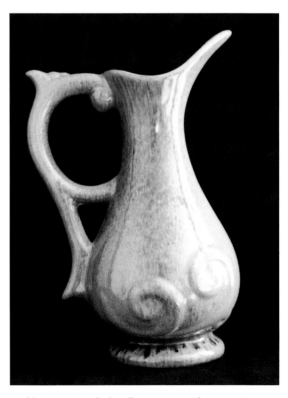

Mold #J-25, Swirled Bulb Bottom Pitcher, 10-7/8" H, Mark: "J-25 Gonder U.S.A.," Script, Sea Swirl. Value: $50-75.

Mold #J-54, Slotted Lizard Handle Pitcher (hard to find), 10-5/8" H x 8-1/2" L, Mark: "Gonder J-54," Script, Wine Brown. *Courtesy of Regina & Al Brown.* Value: $100-125.

Mold #J-54, Slotted Lizard Handle Pitcher (reverse view), Mother Of Pearl. *Courtesy of Rod Emlet.*

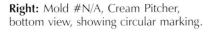

Right: Mold #N/A, Cream Pitcher, bottom view, showing circular marking.

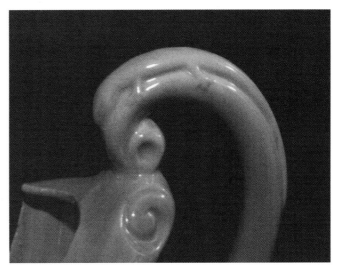

Mold #J-54, Slotted Lizard Handle Pitcher (close up view of handle with lizard), Mother Of Pearl. Courtesy of Rod Emlet.

Mold #N/A, Cream Pitcher, front view (this pitcher was previously unknown until brought to the Gonder Reunion meeting in July 2000), 7-1/2" H, Mark: "Mfd by Gonder For House-Prall Ass'cts PAT: D-16 8-038- Oct 28, 1952," Block, White. *Courtesy of Charles Joray.* Value: $25-30.

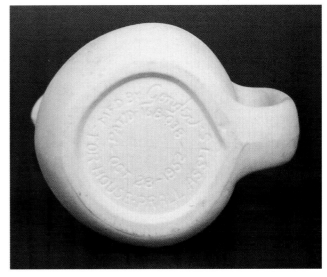

Chapter 16
Planters

Next to the vases produced, Gonder produced more planters than any other form. They include two rare planters, the Mermaid Planter and what we call the Pan Flute Player with Nude Planter. To find either one of these must be considered the Gonder find of a lifetime. Of interest may be the common, small Swan Planter (Mold #E-44), which appears in every glaze combination Gonder issued. One could build a glaze collection with just this simple planter.

Mold #216, Seashell Cornucopia Planter, 6-1/4" H x 10" L, Mark: "Gonder Original 216," Script, Wine Brown. *Courtesy of Rod Emlet.* Value: $70-90.

Mold #221, Mermaid Console Planter. (Very rare. This is the only one of these planters that has surfaced to date. It is one of the most coveted pieces of Gonder.) 7" H x 15-1/2" L, Mark: "221," Block, Red Flambé with White Figurine. *Courtesy of Rod Emlet.* Value: $N/P.

Below: Mold #218 & #213, Side Planters & Doe with Turned Head Figurine, Planters: 2-3/4" H x 3-3/4" W x 3" L; Doe: 10-5/8" H x 3" W x 4-1/2" L, Mark: None, Dijon. *Courtesy of Rod Emlet.* Value, planters: $25-50; Figurine: $50-75.

Mold #237, Reclining Panther Planter (very hard to find), 5-1/2" H x 14-7/8" L, Mark: "Gonder Original 237," Script, Dijon. *Courtesy of Rod Emlet.* Value: $125-150.

Mold #403, 3-Hole Swirl Planter (very hard to find), 8-1/2" H x 3-3/4" W, Mark: None, Yellow. *Courtesy of Rod Emlet.* Value: $75-100.

Mold #519, Comedy/Tragedy Planter (has also been found as a TV Lamp), 7" H x 10-1/2" L, Mark: "Gonder Original 519," Script, Dijon. Value: $75-100.

Mold #510, Hooked Square Single Planter, 2-3/4" H x 3-1/4" W x 5-3/4" L, Mark: "Gonder 510," Script, Celedon Green. *Courtesy of Tom & Dixie Woodward.* Value: $15-25.

Mold #513, Hooked Squares Single Planter (front view), 2-5/8" H x 5-3/4" W x 5-3/4" L, Mark: "Gonder Original 513," Script, White with Brown Swirl. *Courtesy of Regina & Al Brown.* Value: $20-30.

Mold #513, Hooked Squares Single Planter (bottom view). *Courtesy of Regina & Al Brown.*

Mold #550, Small Chinese Junk Planter, 2-3/4" H x 3" W x 10-3/8" L, Mark: "550 Gonder U.S.A.," Script, Forest Green with White Volcanic Drip. Value: $10-20.

Mold #593, Nude with Deer Planter (scarce), 9-1/2" H x 14-3/8" L, Mark: "Gonder Original 593," Script, Rutile Green. *Courtesy of Rod Emlet.* Value: $250-300.

Mold #553, Winged Horse Planter, 6-1/2" H x 4" W x 9-1/4" L, Mark: "Gonder 553," Script, Sea Swirl. Value: $65-85.

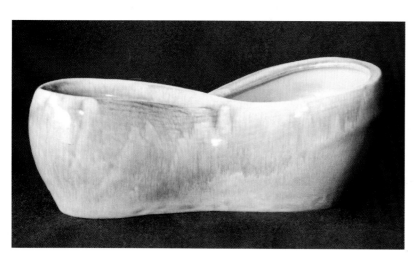

Mold #585, Twist Shoe Strap Planter (hard to find), 4" H x 4-5/8" W x 10-5/8" L, Mark: "Gonder Original," Script, Dijon. *Courtesy of Rod Emlet.* Value: $40-60.

Mold #674, Slanted Basket Planter, 7-3/4" H x 7-3/4" L, Mark: "Gonder Original," Script, Sea Swirl. *Courtesy of Regina & Al Brown.* Value: $25-50.

Mold #692, Shell Cornucopia Planter, 5" H x 9-1/2" L, Mark: "Gonder 692 Original," Script, Red Flambé. *Courtesy of Bernice A. & Ralph H. Baker.* Value, normally: $50-75; with this glaze: $75-100.

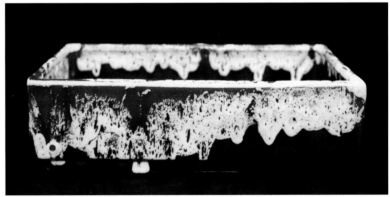

Mold #700, Large Rectangular Planter, 3-1/4" H x 7-3/4" W x 11-1/2" L, Mark: "Gonder Original 700," Script, Victorian Wine with Volcanic White Drip. *Courtesy of Rod Emlet.* Value: $20-35.

Mold #711, Double Footed Planter, 2-7/8" H x 5" W x 8-5/8" L, Mark: "Gonder Original 711," Script, White with Brown Swirl. *Courtesy of Tom & Dixie Woodward.* Value: $15-25.

Mold #716, Double Footed Planter, 2-3/4" H x 4-3/4" W x 8-1/4" L, Mark: "Gonder Original 716," Script, White with raised brushed Green. *Courtesy of Rod Emlet.* Value: $25-40.

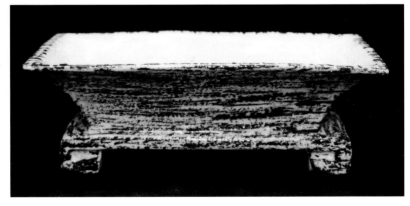

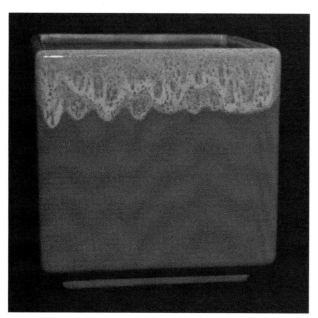

Mold #724, Rectangle Bottom Planter, 3-3/8" H x 4" W x 4" L, Mark: "Gonder 724," Script, Dove Gray with Volcanic White Drip. *Courtesy of Rod Emlet.* Value: $5-10.

Mold #737, Zig Zag Planter, 2-1/2" H x 11-3/4" L, Mark: None, Pistachio with White Volcanic Drip. *Courtesy of Tom & Dixie Woodward.* Value: $15-30.

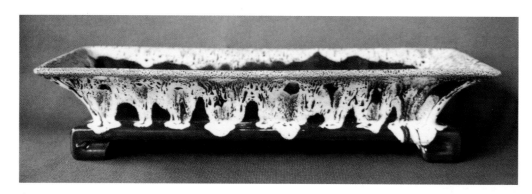

Mold #727, Rectangular Pagoda Planter, 2-3/4" H x 5" W x 12-1/2" L, Mark: "Gonder Original 727," Script, Victorian Wine with Volcanic White Drip. *Courtesy of Rod Emlet.* Value: $25-35.

Mold #733, Square Flared Planter, 2-1/2" H x 6-3/8" W x 6-1/2" L, Mark: "Gonder Original 733," Script, Dove Gray with Volcanic White Drip. *Courtesy of Regina & Al Brown.* Value: $15-30.

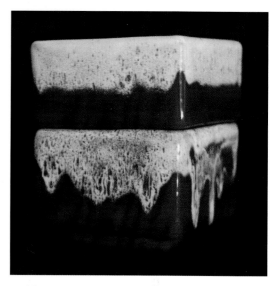

Mold #738, African Violet Planter Set, two piece, side view, 5-1/16" H x 4" W x 4" L, Mark: "Gonder Original 738," Script, Victorian Wine with Volcanic White Drip. Value: $15-25.

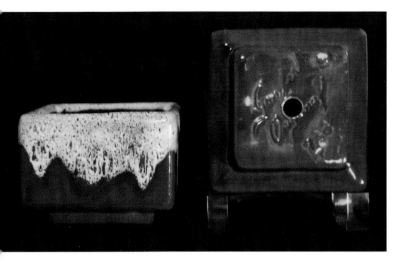

Mold #738, African Violet Planter Set (bottom view, showing hole where wick would be passed through to top plant), 5-1/16" H x 4" W x 4" L, Mark: "Gonder Original 738," Script, Victorian Wine with Volcanic White Drip. Value: $13-18.

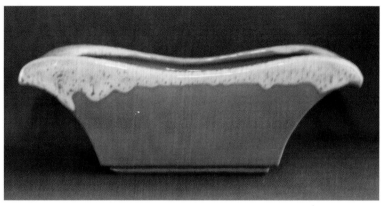

Mold #752, Large Rectangle with Round Corners Planter, 3-1/8" H x 4-1/2" W x 9-1/4" L, Mark: "Gonder Original 752," Script, Dove Gray with Volcanic White Drip. *Courtesy of Regina & Al Brown.* Value: $10-20.

Mold #742, Hexagon Bowl with Chinese Figures Footed Planter, 5" H x 9-1/2" W, Mark: "Gonder Original 742," Victorian Wine with Volcanic White Drip. *Courtesy of Rod Emlet.* Value: $25-40.

Mold #748, Small Flared Square, 4-Footed Planter, 3-7/8" H x 5" W x 5-1/4" L, Mark: "Gonder Original 748," Script, White with Blue Swirl. *Courtesy of Rod Emlet.* Value: $15-30.

Mold #753, Flared Square Pedestal 4-Footed Planter, 7-1/4" H x 7-1/4" W x 7" L, Mark: "Gonder Original 753," Script, Victorian Wine with Volcanic White Drip. *Courtesy of Regina & Al Brown.* Value: $25-40.

Mold #792, African Violet 2-Piece Flared Top Planter, 5-1/8" H x 5-1/4" W x 5-1/4" L, Mark: "Gonder Original 738," Script, Dijon. *Courtesy of Regina & Al Brown.* Value: $20-40.

Mold #800, Wild Mustang Planter, rear view. (Very rare. One of the most phenomenal pieces of Gonder discovered, and the only one found to date; a production number usually means the item was produced, so there may be more. We will have to wait and see.) 13" H x 14" L, Mark: "800 Gonder Original," Script, Forest Green & Red Orange. *Courtesy of Regina & Al Brown.* Value: $N/P.

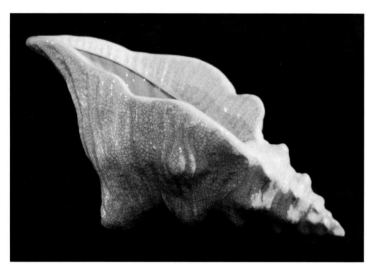

Mold #793, Large Conch Shell Planter (very hard to find), 8" H x 5-3/4" W x 17-1/4" L, Mark: None, Chinese White Crackle. *Courtesy of Rod Emlet.* Value: $200-250.

Mold #800, Wild Mustang Planter, front view. *Courtesy of Regina & Al Brown.* Value: $N/P.

Mold #802, Chuck Wagon Planter (scarce), 6" H x 11-1/2" W, Mark: None, Celedon Green. *Courtesy of Regina & Al Brown.* Value: $100-125.

Mold #1000, African Violet with Ridges & Leaves Planter, 5-1/4" H x 4" W x 4" L, Mark: None, Script, Coral Lustre. *Courtesy of Regina & Al Brown.* Value: $25-40.

Mold #1002, Square with Ridges & Leaves Planter, 5-3/16" H x 5-1/4" W x 5-1/2" L, Mark: "Gonder Original 1002," Script, Dijon. *Courtesy of Regina & Al Brown.* Value: $15-25.

Mold #1001, Square Ridges & Leaves Planter, 3-3/4" H x 5-1/8" W x 5-1/8" L, Mark: "1001 Gonder Orig'l," Script, Forest Green. Value: $15-25.

Mold #1004, Lidded Rectangular with Ridges & Leaves Planter or Dresser Box, 4-1/2" H x 5-1/2" W x 9-1/2" L, Mark: "Gonder Original 1004," Script, Forest Green. *Courtesy of Regina & Al Brown.* Value: $35-50.

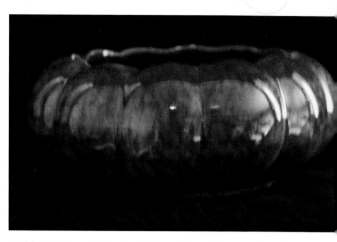

Mold #E-12 or #312, Small Fluted Bowl Planter, 2-13/16" H x 7-1/8" W, Mark: "Gonder U.S.A.," Script, Red Flambé. Value, normally: $5-15; with this glaze: $10-20.

Mold #749/20, Medium Flared Squared 4-Footed Planter. (These are known as "End of Day" pieces, since not many have been found, and they do not appear to have been regular production pieces, even though they were shown in a catalog sheet.) 6" H x 6-1/4" W, Mark: "Gonder Original 749," Script, Matte Brown with Squeeze Bag Decoration. *Courtesy of Rod Emlet.* Value: $40-50.

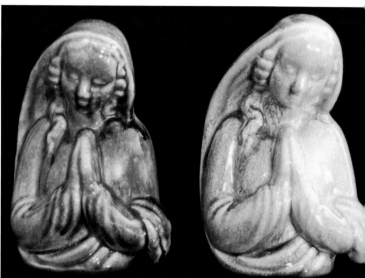

Mold #R-303 (Left) or #E-303 (Right), Madonna Planters, pair. (The R-303 version is an early piece made from a RumRill mold and thus used the RumRill mold number; the E-303 version is a later piece and uses the script marking.) Front view, both: 5-3/4" H x 4" W, Left Mark: "R-303 Gonder U.S.A.;" Block & Right Mark: "Gonder E-303," Script, Left: French Lilac, & Right: Sea Swirl. Value, both: $10-20.

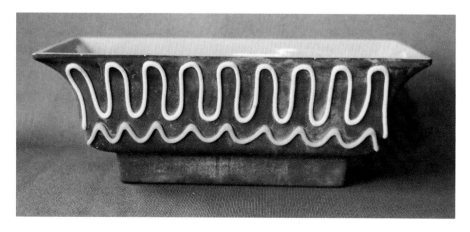

Mold #779/20, Flared Rectangle Footed Planter ("End of Day"), 3-1/2" H x 4-3/4" W x 10" L, Mark: None, Matte Brown with Squeeze Bag Decoration. *Courtesy of Rod Emlet.* Value: $40-50.

Mold #E-44, Small Swan Planter, 5-1/4" H x 3-7/8" W x 5-3/4" L, Mark: "E-44 Gonder USA," Script, Unusual Multi-glaze. Value, normally: $10-15; with this glaze: $15-20.

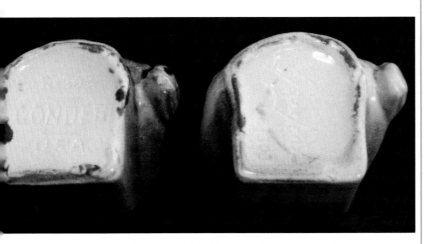

Mold #R-303 (Left) or #E-303 (Right), Madonna Planters (Pair), bottom views.

Mold #E-44, Small Swan Planters, group picture of various glaze colors: top, matte white; bottom, left to right: Ming Yellow, Antique Gold Crackle, & French Lilac. We believe it to be possible to find every Gonder glaze color by collecting these planters, which were produced in every glaze used.

Mold #H-80, Urn with Large Leaf Planter, 6-5/16" H x 7-3/4" W, Mark: "Gonder USA H-80," Script, Coral Lustre. Value: $20-35.

Mold #J-31, Medium Swan Planter (front view), 8-1/16" H x 5-1/4" W x 8-1/4" L, Mark: "J-31 Gonder Made In U.S.A.," Block, Ming Yellow. Value: $30-45.

Mold #H-83, Tab Handle Pot Planter, 5-3/8" H x 6-1/2" W, Mark: "H-83 Gonder U.S.A.," Script, Sea Swirl. *Courtesy of Regina & Al Brown.* Value: $50-60.

Mold #J-31, Medium Swan Planter (bottom view).

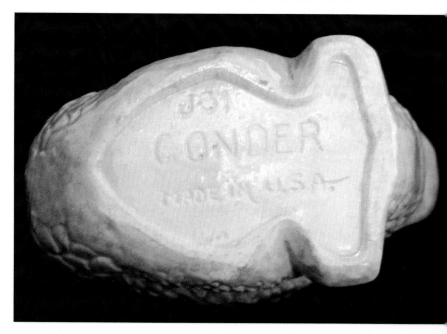

Mold #L-14, Large Swan Planter (hard to find), 8-1/4" H, Mark: "L-14 Gonder U.S.A.," Block, Coral Lustre. *Courtesy of Regina & Al Brown.* Value: $50-75.

Mold #N/A, Oil Lamp Planter, sometimes called the Aladdin Lamp Planter (very hard to find), 2-5/8" H x 11-3/4" L, Mark: "Gonder Original," Script, Red Flambé. *Courtesy of Rod Emlet.* Value, normally: $75-100; with this glaze: $110-150.

Left to right: Mold #L-14, #J-31, #E-44. Shows the various sizes of the three planters when placed side by side.

Above: Mold #N/A, Pan Flute Player & Nude Dancer Planter. (This piece has been found as both a planter and a figurine. It is one of the most desirable pieces of Gonder. We have heard of only 7 or 8 of these pieces being found, and it should be considered Very Rare.) 12" H x 15" L, Mark: "Gonder," Script, Forest Green. *Courtesy of Charles Joray.* Value: $N/P.

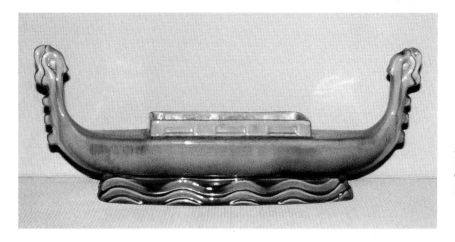

Mold #N/A, Gondola Planter (also seen as a lamp base), 5-3/4" H x 14" L, Mark: None, Jade. *Courtesy of Bernice A. & Ralph H. Baker.* Value $60-80.

Chapter 17
Plaques

While they are out there, these pieces are very hard to find. Some might almost call them scarce. We only know of two Lady Godiva plaques in existence, but more must surely be around. The African mask plaques are just as elusive. There are four of them known, but we have been able to photograph only three of the mold numbers. The catalog pages at the end of the book shows the design of the fourth mask.

Left Mold #231 & Right #232, African Mask Plaques (very hard to find), 5-1/8" W x 8-1/4" L, Mark: "Gonder Original 231," Script, Left: Nubian Black & Right: Gunmetal Black. *Courtesy of Rod Emlet.* Value, each: $75-100.

Mold #222, Lady Godiva Plaque. (Scarce. Only two of these are known by the authors, but more are sure to exist.) 12-3/8" W, Mark: None, Rutile Green. *Courtesy of Regina & Al Brown.* Value: $N/P.

Mold #234, African Mask Plaque, Pair (very hard to find), Mark: "Gonder Original 234," Script, Left: Red Orange & Right: Chartreuse. *Courtesy of Rod Emlet.* Value: $75-100.

Chapter 18
Strainers, Tankards, & Teapots

Only one strainer has been found to date, and it is displayed. The one piece we have been able to identify as a tankard is also displayed. Gonder produced many teapots for the market. Some are in the La Gonda chapter. The ones displayed here are not part of any particular line we have been able to identify. Two of the teapots were previously unknown (Mold #662 & #P-424). These will become welcome additions to any collection.

Mold #N/A, Shaped S&P Salt & Pepper Shakers, 2-3/4" H, Mark: None, Turquoise Green. Value: $5-10.

Mold #971, Tea Strainer, top view. (Only two of these have been found to date, that we know of, thus, we consider it scarce.) 7" W x 5-1/4" L, Mark: "971 Gonder Original," Script, Multi-colored. *Courtesy of Regina & Al Brown.* Value: $N/P.

Mold #971, Tea Strainer, open side view. *Courtesy of Regina & Al Brown.* Value: $N/P.

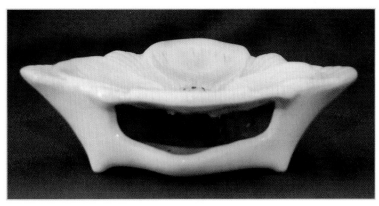

Mold #400, Shell Tankard, left view (very hard to find), 9-1/2" H x 12" L, Mark: "Gonder 400," Script, Victorian Wine over Dove Gray. *Courtesy of Regina & Al Brown.* Value: $150-175.

Mold #M-9, Ribbed Tankard, 14" H x 9" L, Mark: "Gonder U.S.A. M-9," Script, Sea Swirl. *Courtesy of Bernice A. & Ralph H. Baker.* Value: $60-80.

Mold #400, Shell Tankard, right view. *Courtesy of Regina & Al Brown.*

Mold #662, Coiled Beehive Teapot (very hard to find), 5-3/4" H, Mark: "662 Gonder U.S.A.," Block, Light Azure. *Courtesy of Bernice A. & Ralph H. Baker.* Value: $75-100.

Mold #P-31 & #P-33, Round Teapot with Sugar & Creamer: Teapot: 6-1/2" H; Sugar: 4-5/8" H; Creamer: 3-1/2" H; Teapot Mark: "Gonder P-31 USA;" Sugar & Creamer Mark: "P-33 Gonder USA;" Script on all, Yellow with Brown Volcanic Drip. Value, Teapot: $15-25; Sugar & Creamer, both: $15-25.

Mold #P-424, Vertical Ridges Teapot. (Previously unknown teapot. Very hard to find.) 6-7/16" H x 9-5/8" L, Mark: "Gonder P 424," Script, French Lilac. Value: $75-100.

Chapter 19
Tiles & Trays

In 1954, Gonder began conversion of his factory to the production of ceramic tile, and away from art pottery. This conversion was completed by 1955, and only ceramic tile was produced until the factory was sold in 1957. Several designs were used on the tile produced. The examples pictured were the only ones we could find to photograph, but there are others with different designs. The trays are interesting designs within Gonder's production. From large snack trays to small dresser trays, they are functional pieces of Gonder.

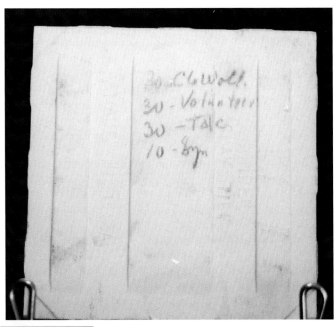

Above: Mold #N/A, Tile, 4-1/2" W x 4-1/2" L, Test Glaze Marked by Hand. *Courtesy of Tom & Dixie Woodward.* Value: $10-15.

Left: Mold #N/A, 3 Tiles, 4-1/4" W x 4-1/4" L, Mark: "Gonder Clay Tile Made in U.S.A.," Block, Maroon, Blue, & Yellow. *Courtesy of Tom & Dixie Woodward.* Value, each: $3-5.

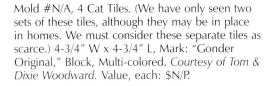

Mold #N/A, 4 Cat Tiles. (We have only seen two sets of these tiles, although they may be in place in homes. We must consider these separate tiles as scarce.) 4-3/4" W x 4-3/4" L, Mark: "Gonder Original," Block, Multi-colored. *Courtesy of Tom & Dixie Woodward.* Value, each: $N/P.

Mold #N/A, Gonder Clay Tiles, 4-3/4" W x 4-3/4" L, Mark: "Gonder Original," Block, Multi-colored. *Courtesy of Tom & Dixie Woodward.* Value, each: $3-5.

Mold #N/A, Gonder Clay Tiles, 4-3/4" W x 4-3/4" L, Mark: "Gonder Original," Block, Multi-colored. *Courtesy of Tom & Dixie Woodward.* Value, each: $3-5.

Mold #100, 8-Section Tray (very hard to find), 1-1/2" H x 10-15/16" W x 19-1/4" L, Mark: "Gonder Original #100," Script, Onionskin. Value: $150-200.

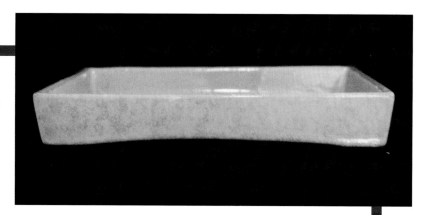

Mold #544, Dresser Tray, side view (hard to find), 1-1/2" H x 7-1/4" W x 10-1/4" L, Mark: "544 Gonder U.S.A.," Script, Coral Lustre. Value: $40-60.

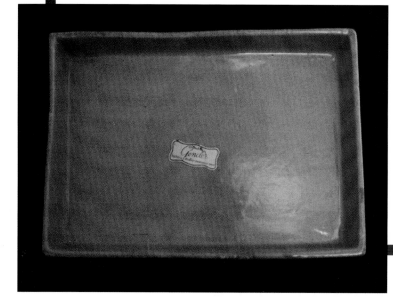

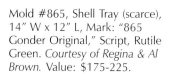

Mold #544, Dresser Tray (hard to find), top view, displaying a paper Gonder label still in the center of the tray.

Mold #865, Shell Tray (scarce), 14" W x 12" L, Mark: "865 Gonder Original," Script, Rutile Green. *Courtesy of Regina & Al Brown.* Value: $175-225.

Chapter 20
Vases

Gonder produced more pieces for their art pottery vase line than for any of their other lines. This was the central reason Lawton Gonder started his own factory. He flourished within the realms of animals, floral designs, elements from the sea, and his beloved Oriental motifs. Many of the vases display what we term "Modern Deco" designs. ("Modern Deco," to Gonder collectors, is a combination of Art Deco with the swirl and modern concepts of design that flourished during the 1950s. Concepts espoused by the designers Rae and Charles Eames were this type of "Modern Deco.") Here Lawton Gonder excelled in glaze combinations and innovative crackle designs. His line of flambé glazes helped win him membership in The American Ceramic Society. These are truly the height of Gonder's design efforts.

Above: Mold #304 or #E-4, Scroll Double Foot Vase, 7-1/2" H x 4-3/8" W x 6-3/4" L, Mark: "304 Gonder USA," Script, Red Flambé. Value, normally: $30-40; with this glaze: $45-60.

Left: Mold #215, Round Gazelle Vase, 9" H x 8-7/8" W, Mark: "Gonder Original 215," Script, Dijon. Value: $50-75.

Below left: Mold #216, Double Horn Vase, 6-1/2" H x 11-1/2" W, Mark: "Gonder Original 216," Script, Unusual Ivory with Blue & Green Sponge. *Courtesy of Rod Emlet.* Value, normally: $50-75; with this glaze: $75-100.

Below right: Mold #360, Ribbed Cornucopia Vase, 6-1/2" H x 6-1/2" L, Mark: "Gonder Original," Script, Green to Yellow. *Courtesy of Bernice A. & Ralph H. Baker.* Value, normally: $20-35.

Mold #361, Olive Branch Vase (hard to find), 5-5/8" H x 4-5/8" W, Mark: "Gonder Original 361," Script, Dijon. Value: $50-75.

Mold #382, Metallic Look Pitcher Vase, 6-1/2" H, Mark: "382 Gonder Original," Script, Dijon. Value: $30-45.

Mold #380, Small Swirl Handle Cornucopia Vase, 5-3/4" H x 6-1/4" L, Mark: "Gonder Original 380," Script, Wine Brown. Value: $25-40.

Mold #383, Bottle with Ridges Vase, 9-3/4" H, Mark: "383 Gonder Original," Script, Antique Gold Crackle. *Courtesy of Regina & Al Brown.* Value, normally: $50-75; with this glaze: $85-125.

Mold #381, Shell Cornucopia Vase, 6-3/8" H, Mark: "Gonder 381 Original," Script, Red Flambé. Value, normally: $20-35; with this glaze: $30-55.

Mold #384, Square Flared Leaves Vase, 5-1/4" H x 5-1/8" W, Mark: "Gonder Original 384," Script, Red Flambé. *Courtesy of Bernice A. & Ralph H. Baker.* Value, normally: $25-35; with this glaze: $35-50.

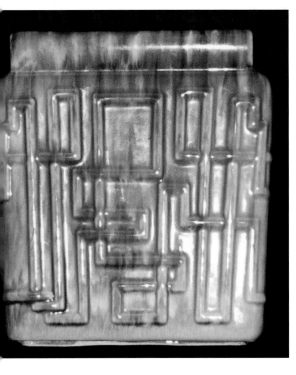

Mold #401, Rectangular Footed Maze Vase, 8" H x 7-1/4" L, Mark: "Gonder Original," Script, Dijon. *Courtesy of Bernice A. & Ralph H. Baker.* Value, normally: $35-50.

Mold #410, Raised Circular Ewer Vase, 8" H, Mark: "410 Gonder Original," Script, Chinese Turquoise Crackle. *Courtesy of Bernice A. & Ralph H. Baker.* Value, normally: $25-40; with this glaze: $35-55.

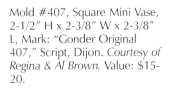

Mold #407, Square Mini Vase, 2-1/2" H x 2-3/8" W x 2-3/8" L, Mark: "Gonder Original 407," Script, Dijon. *Courtesy of Regina & Al Brown.* Value: $15-20.

Mold #418, Drape Vase, 6-1/2" H, Mark: "418 Gonder Original," Script, Dijon. *Courtesy of Regina & Al Brown.* Value: $40-55.

Mold #419, Double Handle Cornucopia Vase,
7-1/2" H x 6-1/2" W, Mark: "Gonder Original
419," Script, White with Antique Gold Crackle.
Courtesy of Rod Emlet. Value, normally: $30-45;
with this glaze: $50-75.

Mold #503, Dolphin Vase, Pair, showing both sides of this unusual
vase.

Mold #503, Dolphin Vase. (Rare. We only know
of 4 vases in private collections, but we are sure
there are others.) 15-1/2" H x 5-1/2" W x 8" L,
Mark: "Gonder 503," Script, Mother Of Pearl.
Value: $N/P.

Mold #504, Multi Fan Leaf Vase with Flowers,
10-11/16" H x 8-1/2" L, Mark: "Gonder 504
U.S.A.," Script, Coral Lustre. Value: $40-65.

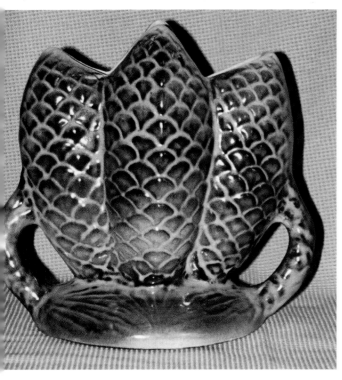

Mold #509, Large Double Shell Cornucopia Vase (scarce), 9-9/16" H x 15-1/4" L, Mark: None, RumRill Green with Brown. (This glaze color is an early glaze left over from production of RumRill pieces, and is not a standard Gonder glaze treatment.) Value: $150-175.

Mold #507, Pine Cone Vase (hard to find), 8-1/2" H x 9" W, Mark: "USA," Block, Greens & Browns. *Courtesy of Bernice A. & Ralph H. Baker.* Value: $65-85.

Mold #509, Large Double Shell Cornucopia Vase (scarce), 9-1/2" H x 12" L, Mark: "Gonder 509," Script, French Lilac. *Courtesy of Regina & Al Brown.* Value: $150-200.

Left: Mold #508, Seashell Ewer Vase with Starfish. (This vase also appears without the starfish at the base, but the same mold number. It was thought that the starfish vase was harder to find, but we have seen more with starfish than without, and thus believe that the vases without a starfish are harder to locate.) 13-3/8" H, Mark: "508 Gonder U.S.A.," Script, Chinese Turquoise Crackle. Value, normally, with starfish: $60-80; with this glaze: $85-110. Value without starfish: $75-100.

Mold #511, Double Hooked Square Vase, 5-1/2"
W x 5-1/2" L, Mark: "Gonder Original," Script,
Jade. *Courtesy of Bernice A. & Ralph H. Baker.*
Value: $40-60.

Mold #512, Triple Hooked Squares Vase, side view (hard to find), 8" H x 5-1/2"
W, Mark: "512 Gonder Original," Script, White with Brown Swirl. *Courtesy of
Bernice A. & Ralph H. Baker.* Value: $75-100.

Mold #512, Triple Hooked Squares Vase, bottom view. *Courtesy of Bernice
A. & Ralph H. Baker.*

Mold #511 or #811, Stylized Swan Vase, 9-1/4" H x 9-3/4"
L, Mark: "Gonder 511," Script, Chinese White Crackle.
Value, normally: $35-50; with this glaze: $45-65.

Mold #513 or #813, Large Double Footed Leaf Vase (front view), 11-1/8" H x 5-5/16" W x 9-1/2" L, Mark: "513 Gonder U.S.A.," Script, Ming Yellow. Value: $40-60.

Mold #513 or #813, Large Double Footed Leaf Vase (bottom view).

Mold #514, Seagull on Piling Vase (very hard to find), 12" H, Mark: "514 Gonder U.S.A.," Script, White on Wine Brown. *Courtesy of Bernice A. & Ralph H. Baker.* Value: $175-225.

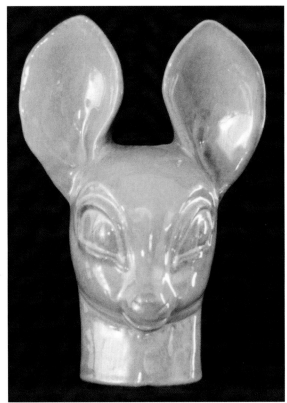

Mold #518, Doe Head Vase (front view), 9-3/4" H x 7" W, Mark: "Gonder U.S.A. 518," Script, Dijon. Value: $50-75.

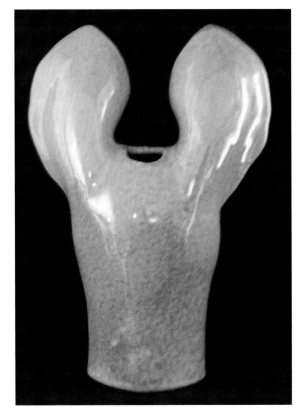

Mold #518, Doe Head Vase (back view).

109

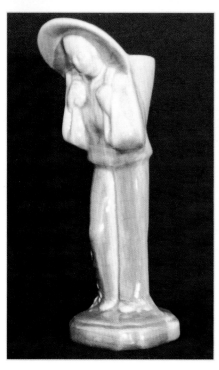 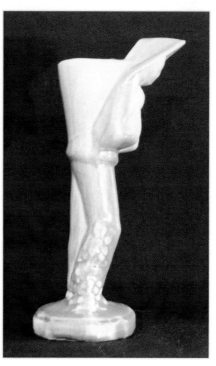

Mold #519, Standing Oriental Male
Vase (left side view), 9" H x 3-1/8" W,
Mark: "USA Gonder 519," Script,
Chinese Turquoise Crackle. Value,
normally: $20-35; with this glaze:
$30-50.

Mold #519, Standing Oriental Male Vase
(right side view).

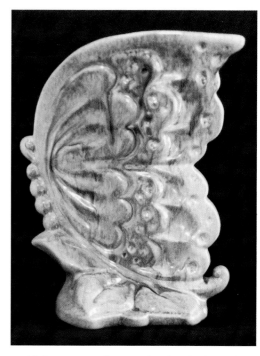

Mold #523, Butterfly Vase (hard to find), 9-3/8"
H x 7" L, Mark: "Gonder 523," Script, Sea Swirl.
Value: $100-150.

Mold #522, Scarla Sunfish Vase (hard to find), 9" H x 1-1/2" W x
10-1/4" L, Mark: "Gonder 522," Script, Lavender. *Courtesy of Rod
Emlet.* Value: $75-125.

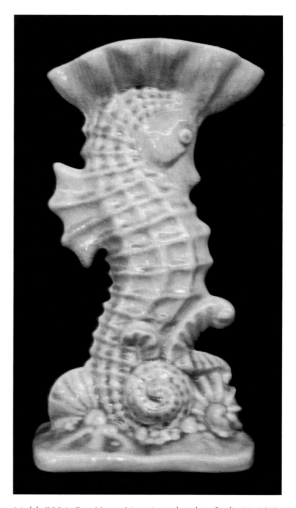

Mold #524, Sea Horse Vase (very hard to find), 11-3/4"
H, Mark: "Gonder," Script, Chinese Turquoise Crackle.
Courtesy of Bernice A. & Ralph H. Baker. Value, normally:
$175-225; with this glaze: $245-315.

110

Mold #526, Pegasus Vase, front view (very hard to find), 10-1/2" H x 9-3/4" W, Mark: "Gonder 526," Script, Turquoise Chinese Crackle. *Courtesy of Regina & Al Brown.* Value, normally: $175-225; with this glaze: $245-315.

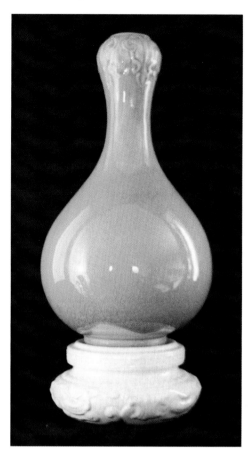

Mold #527 & #527B, Bottle Vase with Base, 9-3/8" H, Mark, Vase: None; Base: "Gonder 527B," Vase: Turquoise Chinese Crackle; Base: White. Value, vase, normally: $75-100; with this glaze: $105-150; base: $25-50.

Mold #526, Pegasus Vase, back view (very hard to find), 9-3/4" H x 10-1/2" W, Mark: "Gonder," Script, French Lilac. Value: $175-225.

Mold #530, Swan Vase, 10-1/2" H x 4" W x 10-5/8" L, Mark: "Gonder Original 530," Script, Red Flambé. Value, normally: $100-125; with this glaze: $150-185.

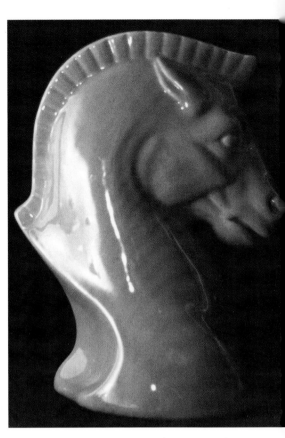

Mold #531, Large Bottle Vase (very hard to find), 18-3/8" H, Mark: "531 Gonder U.S.A.," Script, Antique Gold Crackle. *Courtesy of Regina & Al Brown.* Value, normally: $150-175; with this glaze: $255-300.

Mold #537, Chinese Square with Handles Vase, 8" H, Mark: "537 Gonder," Script, Chartreuse. *Courtesy of Bernice A. & Ralph H. Baker.* Value: $100-125.

Mold #540, Trojan Horse Head Vase, 10-1/4" H x 7-3/4" W, Mark: "Gonder USA," Script, Light Blue. Value: $75-100.

Mold #534, Square Vase with Blocks, 10-1/8" H x 4-1/2" W x 4-1/2" L, Mark: "534 Gonder U.S.A.," Script, Blonde. Value: $50-75.

Mold #539 or #765, Plume Vase, 9-13/16" H, Mark: "539 Gonder U.S.A.," Script, Mother Of Pearl. Value: $50-75.

Mold #559, Cuspidor Top Vase (very hard to find), 7-5/16" H x 8" W, Mark: "559 Gonder U.S.A.," Script, Wine Brown. Value: $200-250.

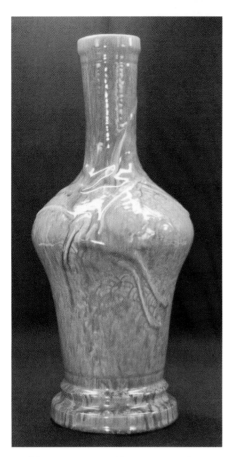

Mold #562, Two Storks Vase, 12-3/4" H, Mark: "Gonder USA 562," Script, Green Agate. *Courtesy of Rod Emlet.* Value: $75-100.

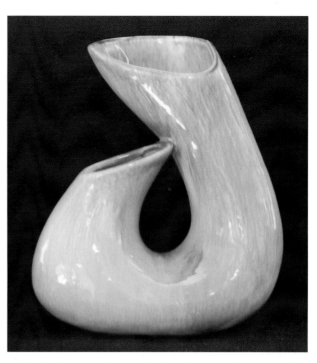

Mold #595, Bent Tube Vase (hard to find), 10-1/4" H x 8-3/4" L, Mark: "Gonder Original 595," Script, Dijon. *Courtesy of Regina & Al Brown.* Value: $75-100.

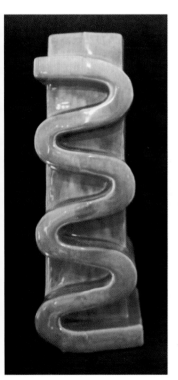

Mold #594, Triple "S" Vase (side view), 11-1/4" H, Mark: "Gonder Original," Script, Red Flambé. *Courtesy of Regina & Al Brown.* Value, normally: $50-75; with this glaze: $75-110.

Mold #594, Triple "S" Vase (front view). *Courtesy of Regina & Al Brown.*

Mold #598, Tall Tapered Vase (hard to find), 14-1/2" H x 4-1/8" W x 6-1/2" L, Mark: "Gonder Original 598," Script, Forest Green. *Courtesy of Regina & Al Brown.* Value: $75-100.

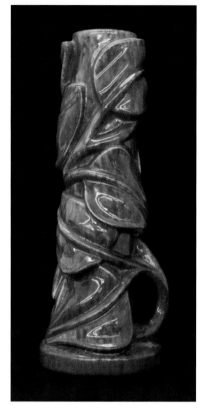

Right: Mold #599, Leaves & Twigs Vase, also seen as a lamp (hard to find), 15-3/4" H, Mark: "Gonder Original 599," Script, Red Flambé. *Courtesy of Rod Emlet.* Value, normally: $100-150; with this glaze: $150-225.

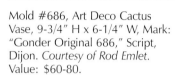

Mold #686, Art Deco Cactus Vase, 9-3/4" H x 6-1/4" W, Mark: "Gonder Original 686," Script, Dijon. *Courtesy of Rod Emlet.* Value: $60-80.

Right: Mold #687, Curved Square Vase with Flower, 8-1/4" H, Mark: "Gonder Original 687," Script, Dijon. *Courtesy of Regina & Al Brown.* Value: $50-75.

Left: Mold #604, Double Open Handles Vase, 9" H x 6-1/4" W, Mark: "#604 Gonder U.S.A.," Script, Antique Gold Crackle. *Courtesy of Rod Emlet.* Value, normally: $75-100; with this glaze: $125-175.

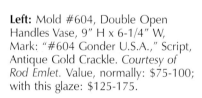

Right: Mold #683, Leaves On Branch Vase, 9-5/8" H x 7" L, Mark: "Gonder Original 683," Script, Dijon. *Courtesy of Regina & Al Brown.* Value: $50-75.

Far right: Mold #688, Square Flower Vase, 8-3/4" H x 4" W x 4-1/4" L, Mark: "688 Gonder Original," Script, Sand. Value: $40-60.

Mold #691, Cornucopia with Leaves Vase, 7-1/2" H x 8" L,
Mark: "Gonder 691 Original," Script, Dijon. *Courtesy of Bernice
A. & Ralph H. Baker.* Value: $50-75.

Mold #704, Large Square Footed Vase,
9-1/4" H x 4-5/8" W, Mark: "Gonder
Original 704," Script, Royal Blue with
Volcanic White Drip. *Courtesy of Rod
Emlet.* Value: $25-40.

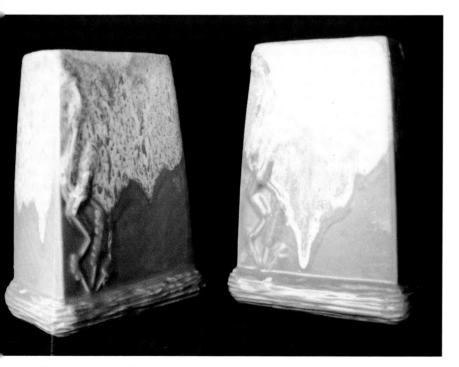

Mold #702, Rectangular Tapered Pillow Vase (Pair), Left: 8-5/8" H; Right: 8-3/4" H
x 6-1/2" W, Mark, Left: "Gonder Original 702;" Right: "Gonder Original," Both:
Script; Left: Dove Gray; Right: Blue with White Volcanic Drip. *Courtesy of Rod
Emlet.* Value, both: $35-50.

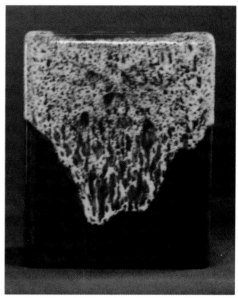

Mold #705, Medium Square Footed Vase, 9-1/4"
H x 2-5/8" W x 5-1/8" L, Mark: "Gonder Original
705," Script, Victorian Wine with Volcanic White
Drip. *Courtesy of Regina & Al Brown.* Value: $10-
20.

Mold #706, Small Square Footed Vase, 4-5/8" H x 4"
W x 4" L, Mark: "706 Gonder Original," Script, Dove
Gray with Volcanic White Drip. *Courtesy of Rod
Emlet.* Value: $10-20.

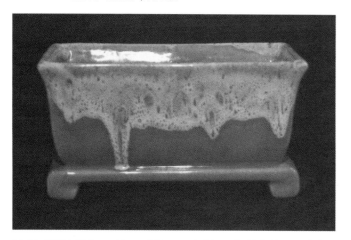

Mold #707, Chinese Footed Rectangle Vase, 3-1/2" H x 3-1/2"
W x 6-3/4" L, Mark: None, Royal Blue with Volcanic White Drip.
Courtesy of Rod Emlet. Value: $15-25.

Mold #708, Large Flat Rectangle Vase, 6-1/2" H x
5" W, Mark: "Gonder Original 708," Script,
Victorian Wine with Volcanic White Drip. *Courtesy
of Rod Emlet.* Value: $15-25.

Mold #710, Small Cylinder Vase, 5-1/4" H x
3-7/8" W, Mark: "Gonder Original 710,"
Script, Yellow with Volcanic White Drip.
Courtesy of Regina & Al Brown. Value: $10-20.

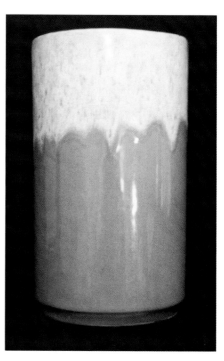

Mold #711, Medium Cylinder Vase, 8-3/8"
H x 4-15/16" W, Mark: "Gonder Original
711," Script, Royal Blue with White
Volcanic Drip. Value: $15-25.

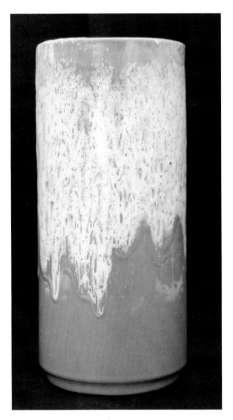

Mold #720 & #726, Chinese Vase with Uneven Handles & Cube Candleholders, Vase: 9-5/8" H x 4" W x 6-3/4" L, Paper Label Mark: "Authentic Chinese Interpretations by Gonder," Block, Black with White Volcanic Drip. *Courtesy of Bernice A. & Ralph H. Baker.* Value, vase: $75-100; candleholders, pair: $20-30.

Mold #712, Large Cylinder Vase, no measurements, Mark: "Gonder Original 712," Script, Royal Blue with White Volcanic Drip. *Courtesy of Rod Emlet.* Value: $25-35.

Right: Mold #745, Small Round Vase, 3-1/2" H, Mark: "Gonder Original 745," Script, Forest Green with White Volcanic Drip. *Courtesy of Rod Emlet.* Value: $15-20.

Mold #750, Large Flared Squared 4-Footed Vase, 7-1/16" H x 6-1/2" W x 6-3/8" L, Mark: "Gonder Original 750," Script, Forest Green with White Volcanic Drip. *Courtesy of Regina & Al Brown.* Value: $25-35.

Mold #720, Chinese Vase with Uneven Handles, 9-5/8" H x 4" W x 6-3/4" L, Mark: "Gonder 720 Original," Script, Chartreuse with White Volcanic Drip. *Courtesy of Regina & Al Brown.* Value: $75-100.

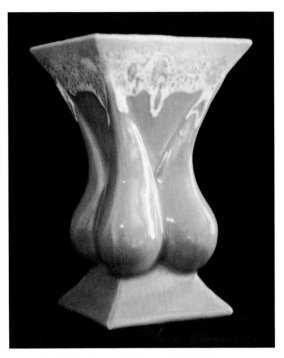

Mold #771 or #E-71 or #E371, Square Bulged Vase, 6-3/16" H x 4" W x 4" L, Mark: "771 Gonder U.S.A.," Script, Dove Gray with White Volcanic Drip. Value: $20-35.

Mold #826 or #K-26, Cactus Vase (front view), 12-3/4" H x 6-5/8" L, Mark: "Gonder 826 U.S.A.," Script, Sea Swirl. Value: $50-75.

Mold #826 or #K-26, Cactus Vase (angled view).

Mold #802, Stylized Swan Vase, 9-3/8" H, Mark: "Gonder Original 802," Script, Sea Swirl. Value: $25-50.

Mold #861, Blades of Grass Vase (hard to find), 11-5/16" H x 9" L, Mark: "Gonder 861 Original," Script, Dijon. *Courtesy of Regina & Al Brown.* Value: $100-125.

Mold #862, Scroll Vase (also seen as a lamp; see lamp section for example), 12-1/4" H x 5" W, Mark: "Gonder Original 862," Script, Red Flambé. Value, normally: $75-125; with this glaze: $110-185.

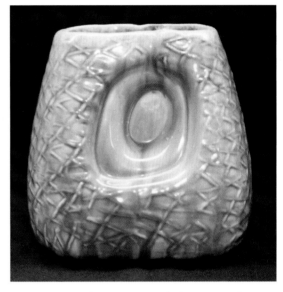

Mold #867, Basket Weave Knothole Vase, 7-1/8" H x 7-1/2" W, Mark: "Gonder Original 867," Script, Dijon. Value: $60-80.

Mold #863, Rounded Square Tall Flowers Vase, 12-1/2" H x 5-3/4" W, Mark: None, Cocoa. *Courtesy of Rod Emlet.* Value: $50-75.

Mold #868, Triangular Double Vase (hard to find), 13-1/16" H, Mark: "Gonder Original 868," Script, Mother Of Pearl. Value: $150-200.

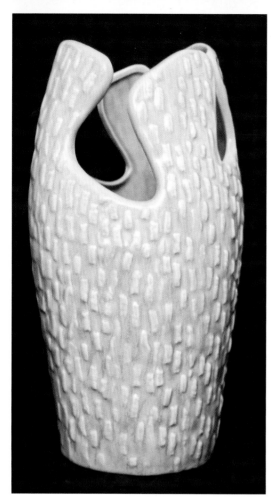

Mold #876, Flared Flower Vase (very hard to find), 10-1/4" H x 9-1/2" L, Mark: "Gonder Original 876," Script, Dijon. Value: $150-175.

Mold #869, Nubby Freeform Vase (very hard to find), 10-3/4" H, Mark: "869 Gonder Original," Script, Turquoise Chinese Crackle. *Courtesy of Bernice A. & Ralph H. Baker.* Value, normally: $150-200; with this glaze: $210-280.

Mold #1203, Raised Circular Bottle Vase, 6-7/8" H, Mark: "Gonder Original 1203," Script, White with Blue Swirl. *Courtesy of Rod Emlet.* Value: $40-60.

Mold #1204, Bottle Vase, 8-1/2" H, Mark: "1204 Gonder Original," Script, White with Brown Swirl. *Courtesy of Regina & Al Brown.* Value: $40-60.

Mold #872, Swirled "S" Handle Vase, with 4-Lips, 10-1/4" H x 5-7/8" W, Mark: "872 Gonder USA," Script, Ming Yellow. Value: $50-75.

Left: Mold #1208, Raised Circular Bud Vase, 7-7/8" H, Mark: "Gonder Original 1208," Script, White with Green Swirl. *Courtesy of Rod Emlet.* Value: $40-60.

Right: Mold #1209, Bottle Vase, 7-5/8" H, Mark: "Gonder Original 1209," Script, White with Brown Swirl. *Courtesy of Rod Emlet.* Value: $50-70.

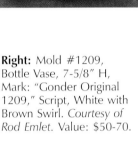

Left: Mold #1210, Bottle Vase, 6-1/8" H, Mark: "Gonder 1210 Original," Script, Red Flambé. *Courtesy of Regina & Al Brown.* Value, normally: $40-60; with this glaze: $60-90.

Right: Mold #1211, Bottle Vase, 8-9/16" H, Mark: "Gonder Original 1211," Script, Red Flambé. Value, normally: $50-75; with this glaze: $75-100.

Mold #E-1, Small Double Handle Vase, 6-7/8" H, Mark: "E-1 Gonder USA," Block, Shell Pink. Value: $10-20.

Mold #E-3, Single Flower Vase (Pair), 7-3/8" H, Mark: "E-3 Gonder U.S.A.," Script, Left: Sea Swirl, & Right: Wine Brown. Value: $10-20.

Mold #E-5 or #305, Small Flat Horn Vase (Pair), 7-3/16" H x 7" L, Mark, both: "E-5 Gonder USA," Script, Left: Antique Gold Crackle & Right: Shell Pink. Value, left: $25-45; right: $15-30.

Mold #E-6, Pinched Center Vase, 7-1/4" H x 3-1/4" W x 5-1/4" L, Mark: "Gonder E-6," Script, Chinese Turquoise Crackle. Value, normally: $15-30; with this glaze: $20-40.

Mold #E-5, Small V Horn Vase, front view. (Until 1999, this vase was only known as a RumRill piece. This piece was brought to a Gonder Reunion meeting and displayed showing the Gonder marking. As such, it is hard to find.), 6-1/4" H, Mark: "E-5 Gonder," Block, Light Blue. *Courtesy of Bernice A. & Ralph H. Baker.* Value: $30-50.

Mold #E-48, Handled Ridged Vase, 6-1/2" H x 4-1/16" W, Mark: "Gonder E-48," Script, French Lilac. (A more traditional Gonder glaze, and a marked piece, defining it as a later production piece.) *Courtesy of Regina & Al Brown.* Value: $10-25.

Left: Mold #E-48, Handled Ridged Vase, 6-1/2" H x 4-1/16" W, Mark: None, Matte White. (With no marking, and with this matte glaze, this piece is probably decorated with a RumRill glaze and was most likely one of the first pieces produced.) Value: $10-25.

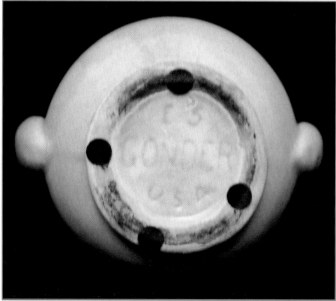

Mold #E-5, Small V Horn Vase, bottom view, showing marking in block letters. This identifies the piece as an early production piece. *Courtesy of Bernice A. & Ralph H. Baker.*

Mold #E-60, Small Fluted Ewer Vase (Pair), 6" H, Mark, both: "Gonder E-60 U.S.A.," Script, Left: Antique Gold Crackle & Right: French Lilac. Value, left: $20-35; right: $10-20.

Mold #E-64, Twisted Vase, 6-1/8" H, Mark: "E-64 Gonder USA," Block, Antique Gold Crackle. *Courtesy of Regina & Al Brown.* Value, normally: $10-20; with this glaze: $15-30.

Mold #E-67, Two Applied Leaf Vase (front view), 6-5/16" H, Mark: "E-67 Gonder U.S.A.," Script, Wine Brown. Value: $20-30.

Mold #E-67, Two Applied Leaf Vase (side view).

Mold #E-65 or #E-365 or #365, Z-Handled Ewer Vase, 6-1/16" H, Mark: "E-65 Gonder USA," Script, Sea Swirl. Value: $15-25.

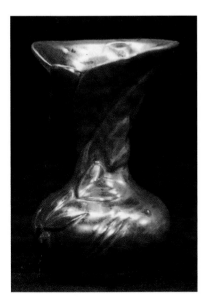

Mold #E-66, Twisted with Leaves Vase, 6-1/4" H, Mark: "Gonder USA E-66," Script, Iridized Gloss over Red Flambé. *Courtesy of Rod Emlet.* Value, normally: $15-30; with this glaze: $20-45.

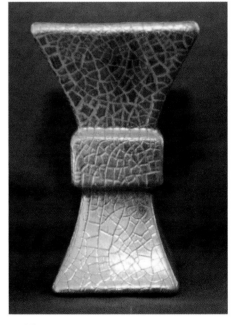

Mold #E-69 or #E-369 or #703, Square Banded Vase, 6-1/4" H x 3-7/8" W x 3-7/8" L, Mark: "E-69 Gonder U.S.A.," Script, Antique Gold Crackle. *Courtesy of Regina & Al Brown.* Value, normally: $20-30; with this glaze: $35-50.

Mold #E-373 or #E-73 or #373, Ribbon Handle Ewer Vase, 6-5/16" H, Mark: "E-373 Gonder U.S.A.," Script, Antique Gold Crackle. Value, normally: $25-35; with this glaze: $40-60.

Mold #E-368, Applied Leaf Vase (Pair), 6-1/4" H, Mark: "E-368 Gonder USA," Script, Mother Of Pearl. Value: $20-25.

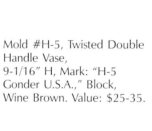

Mold #H-5, Twisted Double Handle Vase, 9-1/16" H, Mark: "H-5 Gonder U.S.A.," Block, Wine Brown. Value: $25-35.

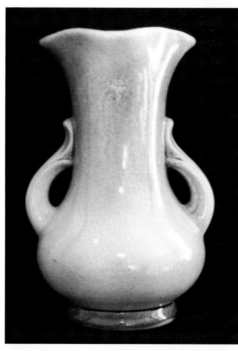

Mold #E-372, Pinched Leaf Vase, 6-3/8" H x 5-15/16" L, Mark: "E-372 Gonder U.S.A.," Script, Antique Gold Crackle. Value, normally: $20-35; with this glaze: $35-60.

Mold #H-7, Square Mouth Double Handle Vase, 8-1/2" H, Mark: "Gonder H-7 U.S.A.," Block, Sea Swirl. Value: $20-30.

Mold #H-14, Shell Cornucopia Vase, 9-1/8" H, Mark: "Gonder H-14 U.S.A.," Block, Sea Swirl (a more traditional glaze treatment). Value: $20-35.

Mold #H-10, Double Handled Flared Vase, 9-1/4" H x 4-1/2" W x 7-7/8" L, Mark: "Gonder H-10," Script, Wine Brown. Value: $15-30.

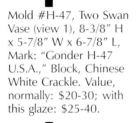

Mold #H-47, Two Swan Vase (view 1), 8-3/8" H x 5-7/8" W x 6-7/8" L, Mark: "Gonder H-47 U.S.A.," Block, Chinese White Crackle. Value, normally: $20-30; with this glaze: $25-40.

Mold #H-14, Shell Cornucopia Vase, 9-3/4" H x 4-1/8" W x 6-3/4" L, Mark: "Gonder H-14 U.S.A.," Block, Ming Yellow with Volcanic Brown Drip. (The mark shows this to be an early piece. The glaze treatment would have been too expensive and time consuming for regular production, so this was either a test piece, or a worker experiment. In either case, not too many of these types have been found, and thus, should be considered of more value.) Value, normally: $20-35; with this glaze: $30-45.

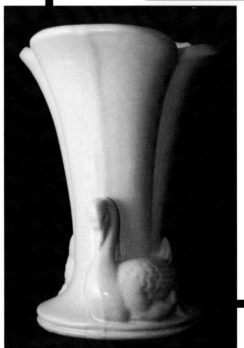

Mold #H-47, Two Swan Vase (view 2).

Mold #H-49, Double Handled Ribbed Vase (Pair), Left: 7-7/16" H x 5-5/8" W; Right: 7-3/4" H x 5-13/16" W (notice that these two are different heights signifying two different molds were used), Mark, both: "Gonder H-49 U.S.A.," both: Block, Left: Mother Of Pearl; Right: Chinese White Crackle. Value, left: $40-60; right: $50-80.

Mold #H-56, Offset Double Handle Vase, 8-1/2" H x 7-1/2" L, Mark: "H-56 Gonder USA," Block, Antique Gold Crackle. Value, with this glaze: $25-50.

Mold #H-55, Berries & Leaves Vase (hard to find), 8-1/16" H x 5-1/4" W, Mark: "Gonder H-55 U.S.A.," Block, French Lilac. Value: $75-100.

Mold #H-56, Offset Double Handle Vase (a very early piece of Gonder found with a RumRill glaze treatment), 8-1/2" H x 7-1/2" W, Mark: "H-56 Gonder U.S.A.," Block, Turquoise. Value, normally: $15-30; with this glaze: $25-40.

Mold #H-62, Swirled Round Double Handle Vase, 9-5/16" H, Mark: "H-62 Gonder USA," Block, French Lilac. Value: $20-30.

Mold #H-67, Triple Leaf Vase, 9-3/16" H, Mark: "Gonder U.S.A. H-67," Block, French Lilac with Brown Volcanic Drip. Value (not a standard production glaze), with this glaze: $35-50.

Mold #H-68 or #668, Large Tulip Vase, 8-7/8" H x 4-5/8" W x 5-7/8" L, Mark: "Gonder H-68," Script, Wine Brown. Value: $15-30.

Mold #H-67, Triple Leaf Vase (showing bottom of another H-67 vase), 9-3/16" H, Mark: "Gonder U.S.A. H-67," Block, Sea Swirl. Value: $15-25.

Mold #H-69 or #669, Half Tulip Vase, 9-1/4" H, Mark: "Gonder U.S.A. H-69," Script, Wine Brown. Value: $25-40.

Mold #H-73 or #673, Medium Ewer Vase, 8-1/4" H, Mark: "H-73 Gonder USA," Script, Red Flambé. Value, normally: $15-30; with this glaze: $20-45.

Mold #H-76, Crane Pillow Vase, 8-5/8" H x 2-7/8" W x 4-3/8" L, Mark: "Gonder U.S.A.," Script, Antique Gold Crackle. Value, normally: $35-50; with this glaze: $60-85.

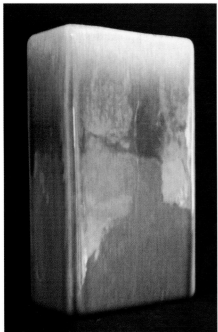

Mold #H-74, Rectangle Pillow Vase, 8-5/8" H x 2-5/8" W x 5" L, Mark: "Gonder U.S.A. H-74," Script, Mocha with Dark Mocha Drip. Value: $15-25.

Mold #H-75, Triple Handle Vase, 8-3/4" H x 5-3/4" W, Mark: None, Coral Lustre. *Courtesy of Regina & Al Brown.* Value: $40-60.

Mold #H-77, Double Handle with Vine Leaves Vase (also seen as a lamp), 8-1/2" H x 7-3/4" W, Mark: "Gonder H-77 U.S.A.," Script, Coral Lustre. Value: $20-35.

Mold #H-78 or #H-478, Flat Multi-Leaf Vase, 8-5/8" H x 2-3/8" W x 5" L, Mark: "Gonder H-78 USA," Script, Dijon. Value: $30-45.

Mold #H-82, Ribbed Fan Vase, 6-3/8" H x 8-1/2" L, Mark: "Gonder H-82 USA," Script, Shell Pink. Value: $25-35.

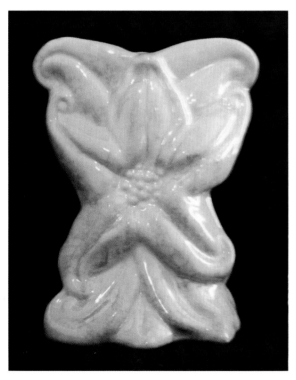

Mold #H-84, Shell Cornucopia Vase, 8-1/16" H x 7-1/2" W, Mark: "H-84 Gonder U.S.A.," Script, Coral Lustre. Value: $25-40.

Mold #H-79 or #H-479, Starfish Vase, 8" H x 6-1/8" L, Mark: "H-79 Gonder USA," Script, Ming Yellow. Value: $15-25.

129

Mold #H-85, Triangle Dolphin Vase, 9-1/16" H, Mark: "Gonder H-85 U.S.A.," Script, Ming Yellow. Value: $40-65.

Below: Mold #H-86 or #H-486, Leaf with Berries Vase, 8-1/2" H x 6-3/4" W, Mark: "H-86 Gonder U.S.A.," Script, Mother Of Pearl. *Courtesy of Rod Emlet.* Value: $20-35.

Mold #H-88, Butterfly with Flowers Vase, 8-5/16" H x 2-7/8" W x 6-5/16" L, Mark: "H-88 Gonder U.S.A.," Script, Ming Yellow. Value: 50-75.

Mold #H-401 or #401, Shell with Seaweed Vase (hard to find), 6-5/8" H x 8" L, Mark: "H-401 Gonder U.S.A.," Script, Mother Of Pearl. *Courtesy of Regina & Al Brown.* Value: $75-100.

Mold #H-87 or #H-487, Peapod Vase, 9" H, Mark: "H-87 Gonder U.S.A.," Script, Wine Brown. *Courtesy of Regina & Al Brown.* Value: $30-40.

Mold #H-601, Knobby Vase, 9-1/4" H x 2-5/8" W x 8-1/8" L, Mark: "H-601 Gonder U.S.A.," Script, Mother Of Pearl with Maroon & Gold Trim Flakes. *Courtesy of Regina & Al Brown.* Value, normally: $35-50; with this glaze & gold trim: $50-75.

Mold #H-603 or #603, Open Center Vase, 9" H x 6-3/4" L, Mark: "H-603 Gonder U.S.A.," Script, Coral Lustre. Value: $35-50.

Mold #H-602, Opposite Leaf Handle Vase, front view (hard to find), 6-3/4" H, Mark: "Gonder U.S.A. H-602," Script, Sea Swirl. *Courtesy of Rod Emlet.* Value: $75-100.

Mold #H-605, Tieback Drape Vase, 9" H x 6-5/8" L, Mark: "H-605 Gonder U.S.A.," Script, Sea Swirl. Value: $50-75.

Mold #H-602, Opposite Leaf Handle Vase, bottom view.

Mold #H-607, Squared Bulbous "Arabian Nights" Vase (hard to find), 9-3/16" H, Mark: "H-607 Gonder U.S.A.," Script, Ming Yellow with Brown Swirls. Value: $125-150.

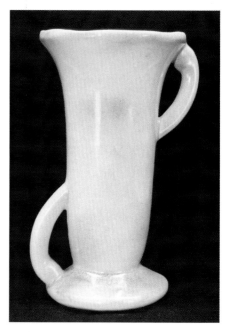

Mold #J-35, Off-Center Double Handle Vase, 10-7/8" H, Mark: "J-35 Gonder USA," Script, Sand. Value: $75-100.

Mold #H-608, Pigtail Handled Vase (hard to find), no measurements, Mark: "Gonder USA," Script, Shell Pink. *Courtesy of Bernice A. & Ralph H. Baker.* Value: $100-150.

Mold #J-57, Lyre Vase, 9" H x 8" W, Mark: "Gonder J-57," Script, Mother Of Pearl. *Courtesy of Regina & Al Brown.* Value: $75-100.

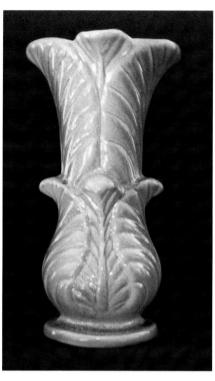

Mold #J-61, Flared Scalloped Shell Cornucopia Vase, 8-9/16" H x 5-1/4" W, Mark: "Gonder J-61 U.S.A.," Script, Mother Of Pearl. Value: $50-65.

Mold #J-59, Round Leaf-In-Leaf Vase, 10-3/4" H, Mark: "Gonder J-59," Script, Wine Brown. *Courtesy of Regina & Al Brown.* Value: $60-80.

Mold #J-60, Shell Fan Vase, 8-1/4" H x 11-1/2" W, Mark: "J-60 Gonder U.S.A.," Script, Wine Brown. Value: $40-55.

Mold #J-64, Cone with Leaves Vase, 9-3/4" H x 7-1/2" W, Mark: "Gonder U.S.A. J-64," Script, Ming Yellow. Value: $40-55.

Mold #J-65, Swan Handle Vase (hard to find), 9-3/8"
H x 5" W x 8" L, Mark: "Gonder," Block, French
Lilac. Value: $100-125.

Mold #J-70, Double Leaf with Berries Vase, 8-7/16" H
x 8-3/8" L, Mark: "Gonder U.S.A. J-70," Script, Mother
Of Pearl. Value: $35-50.

Mold #J-66, Cornucopia Vase with Flat Base, 10" L,
Mark: "Gonder U.S.A.," Script, Mother Of Pearl.
Courtesy of Tom & Dixie Woodward. Value: $25-40.

Mold #J-69 or #869,
Double Curved Handle
Ewer Vase, 9-5/8" H x
3-5/8" W x 8-1/4" L,
Mark: "J-69 Gonder
USA," Script, Antique
Gold Crackle. Value,
normally: $50-65; with
this glaze: $85-110.

Mold #K-15, Peacock Fan Vase, 11-3/4" H x 10-5/8"
W, Mark: "Gonder U.S.A. K-15," Script, Sea Swirl.
Value: $75-100.

Mold #K-15, Peacock Fan Vase (another one, but in a beautiful glaze), 11-3/4" H x 10-5/8" W, Mark: "Gonder U.S.A. K-15," Script, Chinese Turquoise Crackle. Value: $105-140.

Mold #K-25, Swallows Vase, side view.

Mold #K-25, Swallows Vase, front view (very hard to find), 12" H x 5" W x 6-5/8" L, Mark: "Gonder," Script, Coral Lustre. Value: $150-200.

Mold #K-26 or #826, Cactus Vase, 12-1/4" H, Mark: "Gonder USA," Script, Antique Gold Crackle. *Courtesy of Tom & Dixie Woodward.* Value, normally: $50-75; with this glaze: $85-125.

Mold #M-8, Vine Leaf with Flowers Vase. (Hard to find. Usually came with a ceramic base the vase would sit on.) 11-7/16" H, Mark: "Gonder M-8 U.S.A.," Script, Dijon. Value: $75-100.

Mold #M-4, Tall Double Handle Vase (very hard to find), 12-1/2" H, Mark: "Gonder USA M-4," Script, Mother Of Pearl. *Courtesy of Regina & Al Brown.* Value: $125-150.

Chapter 21
Experimental Pieces

More than any other piece of Gonder, collector's will covet an experimental piece that never made it into production. Experimental pieces are usually so rare that no value can be determined for them. These are the few pieces we have been able to find in current collections, and should give collectors an idea of what may be out there. If you are lucky enough to find such a piece, please let us know so that it may be added to the ones known.

Mold #E-14, Fluted Bowl. (An experimental piece made from the candleholder mold, with the candleholder part removed. This now could be used as a nut bowl, or small dresser bowl. The only one currently known to exist.) 1-7/8" H x 4-5/8" W, Mark: "E-14 Gonder U.S.A.," Script, French Lilac with Gold Trim Lip. *Courtesy of Rod Emlet.* Value: $N/P.

Mold #N/A, Experimental, "Merry Christmas 1951" Ashtray. (Made for the 1951 Christmas season, but not produced, for some reason. This is the only ashtray of this type found to date.) Front view, 2-1/4" H x 7-1/2" W x 5-5/16" L, Mark: None, White with Brown. *Courtesy of Tom & Dixie Woodward.* Value: $N/A.

Mold #N/A, Experimental, "Merry Christmas 1951" Ashtray, back view. *Courtesy of Tom & Dixie Woodward.*

Mold #N/A, Experimental, Dog Ashtray. (This piece uses the base ashtray found with the horse head, but substitutes a sitting dog. Never produced, and the only one found to date.) 4-1/4" H x 6-3/4" L, Mark: "Gonder," Script, Brown & Ivory. *Courtesy of Rod Emlet.* Value: N/P.

Mold #N/A, Experimental, Large Egg Bank, side view. (We're not sure what mold this piece was based on. It was probably handmade by a pottery worker as a gift, or could have been a future bank that was never issued.), 3-5/8" H x 6" L, Mark: "Gonder Original," written on top: "Jimmie," Script, Dijon. *Courtesy of Rod Emlet.* Value: $N/P.

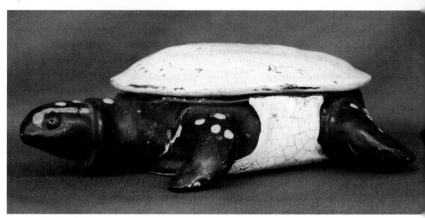

Mold #N/A, Experimental, Turtle Dresser Box, side view. (This piece was rumored for years, but could never be found to verify its existence, until now. Even though this particular piece is rough and has damage, we would guess that any Gonder collector would grab at the chance to own it. An unbelievable find!) 2-3/4" H x 7" W x 8-1/2" L, Mark: "Gonder Original," Script, Brown with Chinese White Crackle. *Courtesy of Regina & Al Brown.* Value: $N/P.

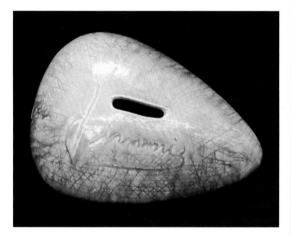

Mold #N/A, Experimental, Large Egg Bank, top view.

Mold #N/A, Experimental, Turtle Dresser Box, bottom view, with top displayed.

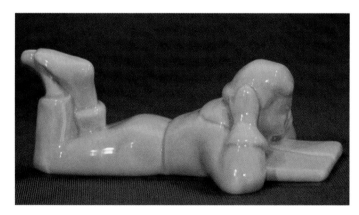

Mold #N/A, Experimental, Boy Reading Figurine, facing right view. (This piece came home with Tom Woodward, Sr., from the Gonder factory. We're sure it was to be part of Gonder's Chinese line of figurines, but never was produced. This is the only one known to exist.) 5-3/4" L, Mark: None, Chartreuse. *Courtesy of Tom & Dixie Woodward.* Value: $N/P.

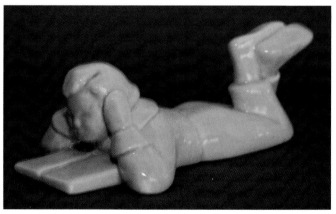

Mold #N/A, Experimental, Boy Reading Figurine, facing left view.

Mold #N/A, Experimental, Buddha Figurine. (The story behind this piece is that it was purchased out of Lawton Gonder's Oriental Room at the factory. It found its way to Columbus, Ohio, where the current owner purchased it in 1990-91. It was said to be a personal favorite of Gonder. It certainly fits the type of Oriental pottery he loved, and may have been a prototype of a future figurine or lamp that was never produced. A monumental piece!) 17-1/2" H, Mark: None, Rutile Green. *Courtesy of Gerald Smith.* Value: N/P.

Mold #N/A, Experimental, Standing Frog Figurine. (A great figurine, in a great custom paint. A few of these have surfaced in different glaze treatments, which fits how an experimental piece would have usually been produced.) 10-1/2" H, Mark: None, Custom Paint on Jade. *Courtesy of Tom & Dixie Woodward.* Value: $N/P.

Mold #N/A, Experimental, Small Frog Figurine, top view. (Another piece brought home by Tom Woodward, Sr., and probably was a future design, or a joke, that was never produced. Once again, this is the only one found to date.) 2-1/2" H, Mark: None, Rutile Green. *Courtesy of Tom & Dixie Woodward.* Value: $N/P.

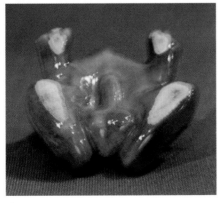

Mold #N/A, Experimental, Small Frog Figurine, bottom view. (This may have been a joke figurine modeled by a factory worker who had a sense of humor. It certainly was a little risqué for the time period it was made.) *Courtesy of Tom & Dixie Woodward.*

Mold #N/A, Experimental, Standing Frog Figurine (another example in a different glaze combination), 10-1/2" H x 8-3/4" W, Mark: None, Pistachio with Black Trim. *Courtesy of Rod Emlet.* Value: $N/P.

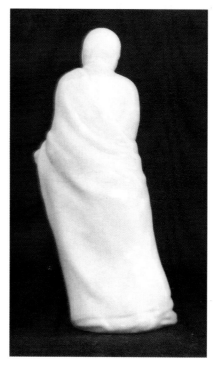

Mold #N/A, Experimental, Greek Man Figurine, rear view.

Mold #N/A, Experimental, Greek Man Figurine, front view. (Purchased in a Zanesville, Ohio, Antique Store, this piece bears all the quality and glaze of a Gonder piece, even without the mark. This is the only one known to exist to date.) 7-1/2" H x 3-3/4" W, Mark: None, Chinese Turquoise Crackle. Value: $N/P.

Mold #N/A, Experimental, Clown Measuring Spoon Holder. (A true experimental piece brought home again from the factory and never produced. We are sure there are others of these, so watch out for them.) 4-1/2" H, Mark: None, White & Green. *Courtesy of Tom & Dixie Woodward.* Value: $N/P.

Mold #N/A, Experimental, Butter Knives, Pair. (An unusual pair of butter knives. Who would have ever thought that Gonder was thinking of expanding into flatware with ceramic handles? Brought home, again, when the decision was made to not produce; they are still something to see. These are the only ones found to date.) 5-7/8" L, Mark: None, White & Cobalt Blue. *Courtesy of Tom & Dixie Woodward.* Value: $N/P.

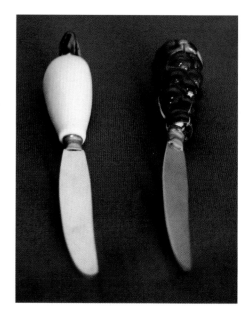

Mold #N/A, Experimental, Stork Figurine. (This piece was, again, brought home by Tom Woodward, Sr., and shows the detail with which Gonder pieces were designed. A true piece of delicate Gonder. It's too bad it was never produced.) 10-1/2" H, Mark: None, Butterscotch. *Courtesy of Tom & Dixie Woodward.* Value: $N/P.

Mold #N/A, Experimental, Jockey Figurine Lamp Base, bottom view showing the markings.

Mold #N/A, Experimental, Jockey Figurine Lamp Base, front view. (First thought to be the only one in existence, another example appeared in an on-line auction in a different glaze. Thus, it appears there may be more out there. A most unusual piece of Gonder.) 14" H, Mark: "Gonder USA," Script, Coral Lustre. *Courtesy of Tom & Dixie Woodward.* Value: $N/P.

Mold #N/A, Experimental, Pinched Pitcher. (Handcrafted by Tom Woodward, Sr., at the factory and brought home. It is unknown if it was a single piece or a potential production piece. We have listed it here for speculation.) 8" H, Mark: None, Red Brown. *Courtesy of Tom & Dixie Woodward.* Value: $N/P.

Mold #N/A, Experimental, Oriental Man & Woman Figurine Lamps. (A beautiful pair of Oriental lamps, a favorite of Lawton Gonder, and the only two ever seen. Perhaps, with this identification, more will surface.) Man: 12-1/2" H; Woman: 12-1/4" H, Marks: None, White with Blue Trim. *Courtesy of Tom & Dixie Woodward.* Values: $N/P.

Mold #N/A, Experimental, Sadiron Planter, standing on edge view. (A wonderful piece displaying the wonderful coral glaze treatment. A potential production planter that has never been seen outside of this example.) No measurements, Mark: None, Coral Lustre. *Courtesy of Tom & Dixie Woodward.* Value: $N/P.

Mold #1285, Experimental, Bud Vase, front view (Shape #1285), 9-1/2" H, Mark: "1285 rest unreadable," Block, Royal Blue. *Courtesy of Rod Emlet.* Value: $N/P.

Mold #N/A, Experimental, Sadiron Planter, front view.

Mold #1285, Experimental, Bud Vase, bottom view showing test markings (Shape #1285).

Mold #221, Experimental, Bud Vase, front view (Shape #221). (This piece shows Gonder's attempt to create a square crystal underglaze pattern, and displays that he succeeded. Why the piece was never produced we don't know, and may never. The only other piece known to exist is in the personal collection of the Gonder family.) 9-5/8" H, Mark: "221-C10-A," Hand-written, Star Pattern under Cobalt Glaze. *Courtesy of Rod Emlet.* Value: $N/P.

Mold #N/A, Experimental, Rosette Draped Vase, view 1 (the only version we have seen, and a particularly beautiful vase), 6-1/4" H, Mark: "E-46 U.S.A.," Block, Rosette. *Courtesy of Regina & Al Brown.* Value: $N/P.

Mold #221, Experimental, Bud Vase, bottom view showing the test markings.

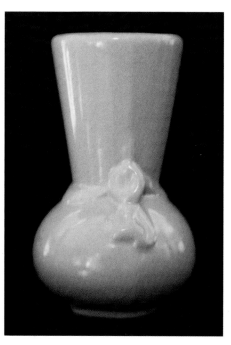

Mold #N/A, Experimental, Rosette Draped Vase, view 2.

Chapter 22
Possible Gonder

Within any collection there will be pieces that the collector believes to be what they collect, but cannot nail down for sure. These are what you will find in this chapter. Some of these pieces have been seen by other collectors and are believed to be good possibilities of inclusion as Gonder products. Others are in personal collections and, until they can be proven to be Gonder or not, will remain in those collections. It is our hope that when others see these pieces, they may be able to verify what they are, or at least concur if they are Gonder or not. Please give us your opinions.

Mold #N/A, Coffee Mug, 1953 Commemorative, Tom Woodward Broken Leg. (This mug was a gift to Tom Woodward, Sr., by fellow workers after he broke his leg in a 1953 accident. We are not sure if it was made at the factory, or just accented and fired prior to the award being given.) 6-1/8" H, Mark: None, White with Gold Trim. *Courtesy of Tom & Dixie Woodward.* Value: $N/P.

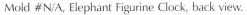

Mold #N/A, Elephant Figurine Clock, back view.

Mold #N/A, Elephant Figurine Clock, front view. (This clock is just too good to be true. It meets every Gonder rule, from the form to the glaze, but no proof or rumor exists that Gonder ever made such a piece. As such, it is placed into this category until proven otherwise. And the clock works, too.) 9-3/8" H x 4-1/8" W x 12-7/8" L, Mark: None, Sea Swirl. Value: $N/P

Far left: Mold #N/A, Anthony Figurine. (This figurine, along with Cleopatra, has been speculated to be Gonder for some time. A few serious collectors have held onto the two figures until proof can be found.) No measurement, Mark: None, except for "ANTHONY" raised on the front bottom, Chartreuse with Gold Trim. *Courtesy of Regina & Al Brown.* Value: $N/P.

Left: Mold #N/A, Cleopatra Figurine. (This figurine, along with Anthony, has been speculated to be Gonder for some time. A few serious collectors have held onto the two figures until proof can be found.) 12-3/8" H x 5-1/8" W x 5-3/4" L, Mark: None, except for "CLEOPATRA" raised on the front bottom, Chartreuse with Gold Trim. Value: $N/P.

Below: Mold #N/A, Two Gazelles Lamp. (Gonder or Haeger? The glaze appears to be a Gonder type. You tell us.) 14-1/4" H, Mark: None, Chartreuse. *Courtesy of Bernice A. & Ralph H. Baker.* Value: $N/P.

Mold #N/A, Double Floral Open Square Lamp. (The glaze is right, and the form design is similar to other Gonder Lamp forms. Still a question.) 9-3/8" H, Mark: None, Victorian Wine. *Courtesy of Rod Emlet.* Value: $N/P.

Mold #N/A, Horse Head Lamp. (This lamp has appeared in an old advertisement for the Howell Lamp Company, dated 1956. This date would place it after Gonder production of art pottery or lamps. During this time, all production had switched to tile manufacturing. Could it be that Gonder had many of these lamps in storage and sold them to Howell to get rid of old inventory? We do not know, since the ad also shows a clock to go with two of the lamps as a set. Until further proof is found, we cannot list this as certified Gonder.)
8-1/2" H, Mark: None, Light Blue with Gold Trim. *Courtesy of Rod Emlet.* Value: $N/P.

Below left: This advertisement from the Howell Lamp Company shows the previous lamp as a set with a clock, all in the same glaze. Until someone can find evidence verifying who produced this lamp, we cannot certify it as Gonder.

Below right: Mold #N/A, Framed Oak Leaves Lamp. (We have never seen Gonder use an oak leaf and acorn motif design, but that doesn't mean he didn't. Proof is needed to determine the final answer.) 9" H, Mark: None, Pistachio. *Courtesy of Rod Emlet.* Value: $N/P.

Right: Mold #N/A, Modern Tapered Lamp (fits the mold design and color), 9" H, Mark: None, Forest Green. *Courtesy of Bernice A. & Ralph H. Baker.* Value: $N/P.

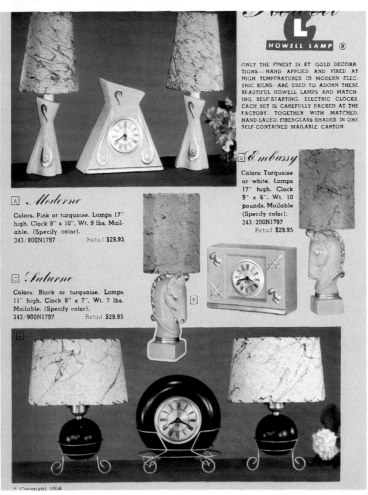

Left: Mold #N/A, Panther On Rock Base Lamp. (This lamp had been previously identified as Gonder, but questions have now risen about that identification. This glaze combination is quite striking and appears to be an individual effort.) 9-5/8" H, Mark: None, Tans & Greens. *Courtesy of Rod Emlet.* Value: $N/P.

Right: Mold #N/A, Mask Wall Pocket. (Although Gonder made a few wall pockets, we have no information that would allow us to identify this example as one. It certainly fits the mask plaque designs that are marked and known as Gonder pieces. Until further proof is received, it will be shown as a "possible.") 5-7/8" W x 9" L, Mark: None, Forest Green. *Courtesy of Rod Emlet.* Value: $N/P.

Mold #N/A, Panther On Rock Base Lamp. (Another version of the same lamp, reverse view, in a different glaze.) 9-3/4" H x 6-3/4" W, Mark: None, Gunmetal Black. Value: $N/P.

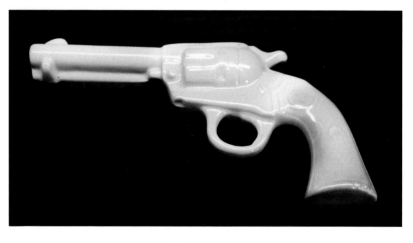

Mold #N/A, Pistol Wall Pocket, back view.

Below: Mold #N/A, Pistol Wall Pocket, front view. (This piece was sold to the current owner by a former Gonder worker, who claimed it was Gonder. However, we can find no verification that such a piece was produced. Until something can be found to verify the claim, it will remain in this section.) 4-1/2" W x 9" L, Mark: "PAT-PND," Pink, Blue, Lavender. *Courtesy of Rod Emlet.* Value: $N/P.

Mold #N/A, Pyramid Floral Lamp. (Right glaze color and style. Unknown as a true Gonder designed lamp.) 12-3/4" H, Mark: None, Victorian Wine. *Courtesy of Rod Emlet.* Value: $N/P.

Chapter 23
Catalog Sales Pages

The following series of pages display actual Gonder Ceramic Arts and Bradley Manufacturing Company catalog sales pages. These pages were probably sent out to clients, or carried by salesmen to show prospective clients what the products looked like. They also displayed the mold number, which was used to place an order for each particular piece.

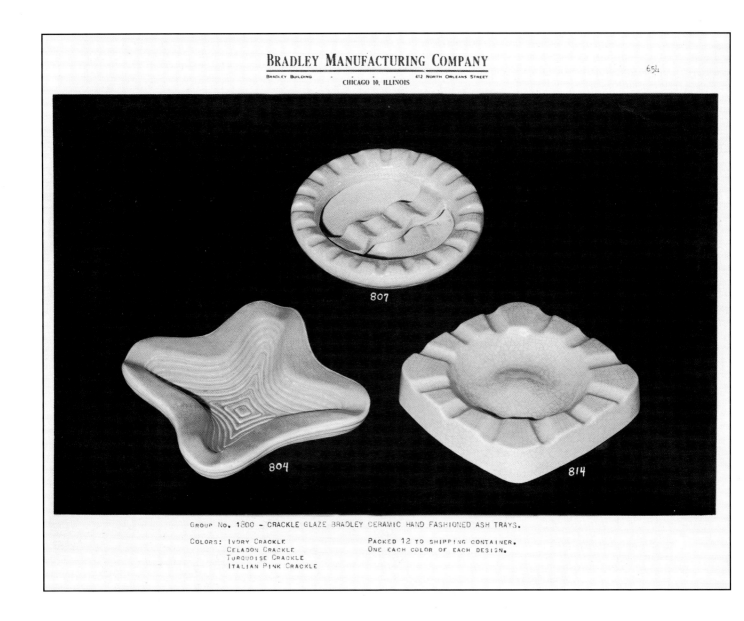

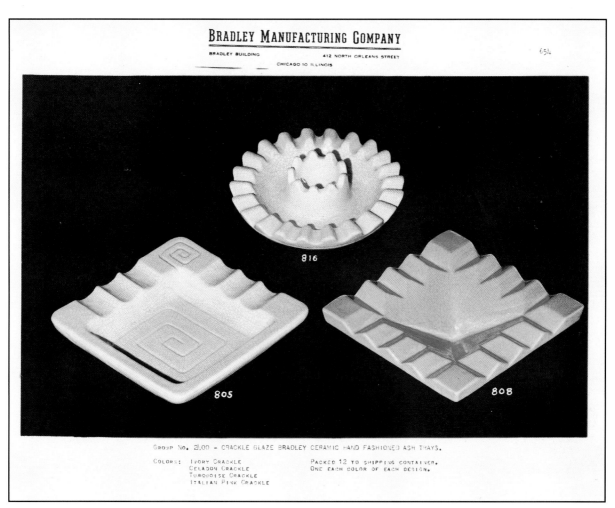

816

805

808

GROUP NO. 2100 - CRACKLE GLAZE BRADLEY CERAMIC HAND FASHIONED ASH TRAYS.

COLORS: IVORY CRACKLE   PACKED 12 TO SHIPPING CONTAINER.
         CELADON CRACKLE   ONE EACH COLOR OF EACH DESIGN.
         TURQUOISE CRACKLE
         ITALIAN PINK CRACKLE

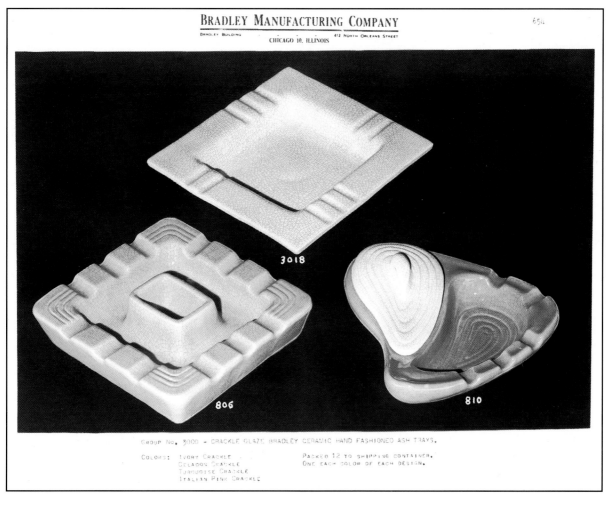

3018

806

810

GROUP NO. 3000 - CRACKLE GLAZE BRADLEY CERAMIC HAND FASHIONED ASH TRAYS.

COLORS: IVORY CRACKLE   PACKED 12 TO SHIPPING CONTAINER.
         CELADON CRACKLE   ONE EACH COLOR OF EACH DESIGN.
         TURQUOISE CRACKLE
         ITALIAN PINK CRACKLE

303 304 305 312 365

369 370 371 373 380 381

400 401 402 403 404

405 406 set 407 set 408

419 414 pc. 409 567 568

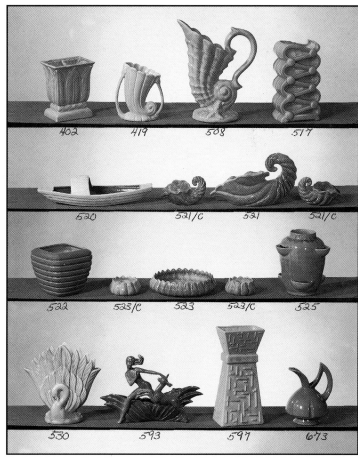

402 419 508 517

520 521/C 521 521/C

522 523/C 523 523/C 525

530 593 597 673

153

GONDER Ceramic Arts

733 727 740 745

748 749 752

909 917 cr. 923 sugar 924

765 208 753

748 749 755 793

792 860 861 863

909 917 993 994 996

803 825 851

754 755 756 583 586

810 811 813 860

869 872 876

GONDER CERAMIC ARTS, Inc.
ZANESVILLE, OHIO

763   765

785   766

1800   1802   1801

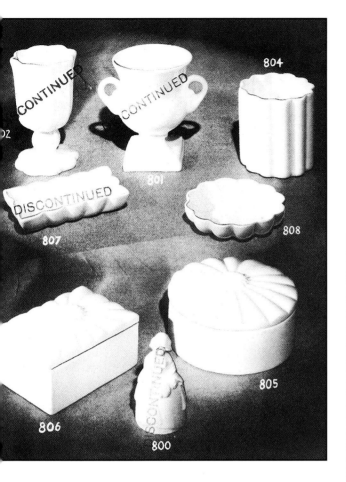

804

CONTINUED

CONTINUED

02

801

DISCONTINUED

807

808

DISCONTINUED

805

806

800

BRADLEY MANUFACTURING COMPANY

BRADLEY BUILDING   •   •   412 NORTH ORLEANS STREET

CHICAGO 10, ILLINOIS

No. 3030
GREEN
WINE
GREY (W/RED SHADE)
HEIGHT: 20"

No. 3031
GREEN
CHARTREUSE
WHITE (W/RED SHADE)
HEIGHT: 20"

No. 1219
GREEN (W/WHITE SHADE)
WINE (W/WHITE SHADE)
WHITE (W/WHITE SHADE)
HEIGHT: 24½"

No. 1226
GREEN
BROWN
GREY
HEIGHT: 24½"

No. 2224
WHITE
CHARTREUSE
BLACK (W/RED SHADE)
HEIGHT: 28"

No. 2227
WHITE (W/RED SHADE)
BLACK (W/WHITE SHADE)
GREEN (W/WHITE SHADE)
HEIGHT: 28"

No. 2228
GREY
GREEN
WHITE
HEIGHT: 28"

No. 2235
WHITE
GREEN
WINE
HEIGHT: 28"

BRADLEY MANUFACTURING COMPANY

BRADLEY BUILDING • • • **412 NORTH ORLEANS STREET**

CHICAGO 10, ILLINOIS

No. 4093
WHITE (w/white shade)
BLACK (w/white shade)
GREEN (w/white shade)
HEIGHT: 30½"

No. 4057
WHITE (w/white shade)
CHARTREUSE (w/white shade)
BLACK (w/white shade)
HEIGHT: 30½"

No. 4094
WHITE CRACKLE (w/white shade) – TURQUOISE CRACKLE (w/white shade)
ROSE CRACKLE (w/white shade) – HEIGHT: 28"

No. 3092
GREEN
BLACK (w/red shade)
GREY (w/red shade)
HEIGHT: 20"

No. 5096 – GREEN – BLACK (w/red shade) –
GREY (w/red shade) – HEIGHT: 16"

No. 3092
GREEN
BLACK (w/red shade)
GREY (w/red shade)
HEIGHT: 20"

No. 3063
REEN (w/white shade)
SREY (w/white shade)
BROWN (w/white shade)
HEIGHT: 20"

No. 5098 – GREEN (w/white shade)
GREY (w/white shade) – BROWN (w/white shade) – HEIGHT: 16"

No. 3063
GREEN (w/white shade)
GREY (w/white shade)
BROWN (w/white shade)
HEIGHT: 20"

BRADLEY MANUFACTURING COMPANY
Bradley Building　-　412 North Orleans Street
CHICAGO 10, ILLINOIS

No. 2255

BLACK W/RED SHADE
CHARTREUSE W/MATCHING SHADE
FOREST GREEN W/MATCHING SHADE

No. 2268

BLACK W/RED SHADE
WINE W/NATURAL SHADE
DOVE GREY W/GREY SHADE

No. 2259

BLACK W/RED SHADE
CHARTREUSE W/MATCHING SHADE
FOREST GREEN W/MATCHING SHADE

SUPERBLY GLAZED BRADLEY CERAMICS IN BRILLIANT TONES. SHADES MADE OF GENUINE
COLORED BRAD-GLO, HIGHLY TRANSLUCENT (RED SHADE ON BLACK BASE). HEIGHT 27½".

BRADLEY MANUFACTURING COMPANY
Bradley Building　-　412 North Orleans Street
CHICAGO 10, ILLINOIS

No. 3060

JADE W/JADE DESIGN
COCOA W/COCOA DESIGN
ROSEWOOD W/ROSEWOOD DESIGN
PISTACHIO W/PISTACHIO DESIGN

HEIGHT: 23½"

No. 3062

BLACK W/RED SHADE
DOVE GREY W/MATCHING SHADE
CHARTREUSE W/MATCHING SHADE
FOREST GREEN W/CHARTREUSE SHADE

HEIGHT: 23½"

No. 3061

COCOA W/AMBER SHADE
ROSEWOOD W/MATCHING SHADE
PISTACHIO W/CHARTREUSE SHADE
GREEN AGATE W/CHARTREUSE SHADE

HEIGHT: 23½"

SUPERBLY GLAZED BRADLEY CERAMICS WITH POLYPLASTEX SHADES AS SHOWN

BRADLEY MANUFACTURING COMPANY

BRADLEY BUILDING · 412 NORTH ORLEANS STREET
CHICAGO 10, ILLINOIS

No. 3067 VANITY UNIT

HEIGHT OF UNIT: 18½".

No. 5087 HOLLYWOOD HEADBOARD UNIT
(RECTANGLE SHADE—ROUND END—19" LONG)
HEIGHT OF UNIT: 16".

No. 3067 VANITY UNIT

HEIGHT OF UNIT: 18½".

COLORS OF #3067 AND #5087
RUTILE GREEN W/WHITE SHADE
MATTE WHITE W/WHITE SHADE

MATTE GLAZE BRADLEY CERAMICS IN
BEAUTIFUL CONTEMPORARY TONES.
LAMINATED VELON SHADE; HAND LACED

BRADLEY MANUFACTURING COMPANY

BRADLEY BUILDING · 412 NORTH ORLEANS STREET
CHICAGO 10, ILLINOIS

No. 3064 VANITY UNIT
(DEEP CONE SHADE)
HEIGHT: 18".

No. 5099 HOLLYWOOD HEADBOARD UNIT
(RECTANGLE SHADE—ROUND END—
19" LONG) HEIGHT: 15½".

No. 3064 VANITY UNIT
(DEEP CONE SHADE)
HEIGHT: 18".

COLORS OF #3064 AND #5099
WHITE W/MATCHING SHADE
BLONDE W/MATCHING SHADE
CHARTREUSE W/MATCHING SHADE

SUPERBLY GLAZED BRADLEY CERAMICS
WITH HAND LACED GENUINE FIBREGLASS
SHADES AS SHOWN.

No. 3088 VANITY UNIT
(DEEP CONE SHADE)
HEIGHT OF UNIT: 17½"

No. 5094 HOLLYWOOD HEADBOARD UNIT
(RECTANGLE SHADE - 18" LONG)
HEIGHT OF UNIT: 16½"

No. 3088 VANITY UNIT
(DEEP CONE SHADE)
HEIGHT OF UNIT: 17½"

COLORS OF #3088 AND #5094
SAND W/MATCHING SHADE
CHARTREUSE W/MATCHING SHADE
VICTORIAN WINE W/RED SHADE

SUPERBLY GLAZED BRADLEY CERAMICS WITH
HAND LACED GENUINE POLYPLASTEX SHADES
AS SHOWN.

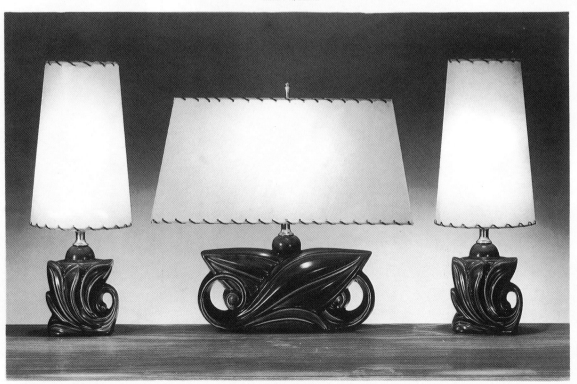

No. 3090 VANITY UNIT
(DEEP CONE SHADE)
HEIGHT OF UNIT: 17½"

No. 5095 HOLLYWOOD HEADBOARD UNIT
(RECTANGLE SHADE - 18" LONG)
HEIGHT OF UNIT: 16½"

No. 3090 VANITY UNIT
(DEEP CONE SHADE)
HEIGHT OF UNIT: 17½"

COLORS OF #3090 AND #5095
GREY W/MATCHING SHADE
PEBBLE W/MATCHING SHADE
FOREST GREEN W/CHARTREUSE SHADE

SUPERBLY GLAZED BRADLEY CERAMICS WITH
HAND LACED GENUINE POLYPLASTEX SHADES
AS SHOWN.

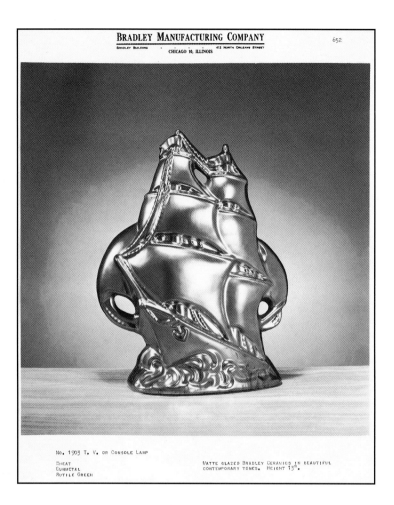

No. 1903 T. V. or Console Lamp

Wheat
Gunmetal
Rutile Green

Matte glazed Bradley Ceramics in beautiful contemporary tones. Height 13".

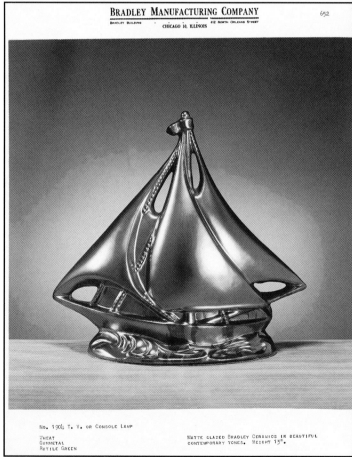

No. 1904 T. V. or Console Lamp

Wheat
Gunmetal
Rutile Green

Matte glazed Bradley Ceramics in beautiful contemporary tones. Height 13".

Chapter 24
Missing Mold Numbers

The following mold numbers and descriptions represent items that could not be found to be photographed for this book. Among the collections we did photograph, we may have missed some of these. If you, the reader, have some of these pieces, please contact the authors. It may be possible to update this book in the future and add some of these pieces to the new update.

70	Planter, Conch Shell	507	Holder, Toothbrush	701	Planter, Rectangular, Small
106	Bowl, Fish Shaped	510	Vase, Flame (810)	703	Vase, Square Banded (E-69)
208	Console Set, Cornucopia (521)	517	Vase, Zigzag & Buttons	709	Vase, Rectangle, Flat, Medium
208	Figurine, Cat, Modern (521)	520	Planter, Chinese Junk, Large	709-A	Vase, Rectangle, Flat, Small
210-A	Planter, Curved Rocky	522	Planter, Square, Horizontal Ridged	710	Vase, Octagon
216/c	Candleholders, Seashell Cornucopia	523/C	Candleholder, Lotus, Round Scallop	712	Bowl, Triangle Nut
217	Vase, Seashell	525	Jar, Strawberry	713	Bowl, Footed, Round
221/c	Candleholders, Mermaid	531-B	Base For 531	717	Vase, Cloverleaf
225	Ashtray, Bowl	534-B	Base For 534	718	Vase, Chinese, Square, with Handles (537)
226	Ashtray, Bowl, Flat	535	Vase, Chinese, Dragon Handle	721	Planter, Quarter Circle
227	Ashtray, Bird, Small	554	Bowl, Fish Face	722	Ashtray, Square, Ridged Top, 7.5"
228	Ashtray, Square Open Center	558	Vase, Fishes	723	Ashtray, Cigar, Elliptical, 5"
229	Ashtray, Tic Tac Toe	566	Vase, Sculpted, Double Form	728	Box, Lidded Cigarette
230	Ashtray, Bird, Large	567	Ashtray, Fish, Small, Spiked Edges	729	Ashtray, Large Cigar
233	Plaque, African Mask	568	Ashtray, Oblong , Small	731	Candleholder, Round
235	Ashtray, Bowling	571	Figurine, Oriental Male, Bald, Swaying	732	Planter, Rectangular Flared
238	Planter, Elephant			734	Planter, Small Square
251	Ashtray, Golf	572	Figurine, Oriental Male, Bearded, on Square Base	735	Planter, Medium Square
303	Vase, Flower (E-3)			736	Planter, Large Square
305	Vase, Horn, Flat (E-5)	576-?	Figurine, Horse Head, 13"	740	Planter, African Violet, Square Set
312	Planter, Bowl, Small Fluted (E-12)	583	Figurine, Horse, Ridged Mane, Open Mouth	741	Bowl, Six-Sided
314	Candleholder, Fluted (414, E-14)			743	Bowl, Square On Pedestal
362	Vase, Leaf, Double Handle High-Low	584	Figurine, Large Robed Oriental Female	746	Vase, Round, Medium
				747	Vase, Round, Large
365	Vase, Ewer, Z-Handled (E-65)	585	Figurine, Large Robed Oriental Male	749	Planter, Flared Squared, 4-Footed, Medium
368	Bottle, Leaf, Applied				
369	Vase, Square Banded (E-69)	586	Figurine/Lamp, Giraffe Head	751	Planter, Rectangle with Round Corners, Small
370	Vase, Leaf, Applied (E-70)	587	Ashtray, Rectangular, Cigar		
371	Vase, Square Bulged (E-71)	589	Ashtray, Reverse "G"	754	Vase, Large Tall Square, Single Band
372	Vase, Leaf, Pinch (E-372)	592	Dish, Dog Bone, Flat	755	Vase, Medium Tall Square, Single Band
373	Pitcher, Fluted Handle (E-73, E-373)	596	Vase, Leaves, Square Open Triple, 11.5"		
				756	Vase, Chinese, Square with Double Handles, 15"
375	Ashtray, Leaf, Flat	597	Vase, Maze, Rectangular, Flared Top & Bottom		
389	Vase, Pineapple			765	Vase, Plume (539)
401	Vase, Shell & Twigs (H-401)	597	Vase, Swirl, Open Triple	779	Planter, Flared Rectangle, Footed
402	Vase, Lotus, Flat	599	Bowl, Console, Rectangular, Double Footed	781	Planter, Madonna, Standing
405	Ashtray, Swirl, with Cup Holder			785	Figurine Planters, Indian Man/Woman with Reed Baskets
407	Ashtray, Set, 4 Square with Square Cigarette Holder	599/c	Candleholders, Rectangular, Double Footed		
				791	Planter, Square, African Violet, Bottom
409	Ashtray, Snow Footprint	601	Vase, Knobby, Flared Top		
411	Ashtray, Triangle	602	Planter, Leaf Handled Pot	792	Planter, 2-Piece Flared Top, African Violet
414	Candleholder, Fluted (314, E-14)	605	Vase, Drape, Tieback (H-605) (Original Label)		
419	Basket, Fluted, Large (L-19)			803	Planter, Sovereign Plain
478	Vase, Leaf, Flat (H-78)	606	Vase, Ewer with Question Mark Handle. (H-606)	804	Ashtray, 4-Point Star
479	Vase, Starfish (H-79)			805	Box, Sovereign Powder
486	Vase, Leaves, Freeform, Molded Base	608	Vase	806	Ashtray, Square with Center Holder
		629	Bowl, Fluted, Large (H-29)	806	Box, Sovereign Cigarette with Lid
487	Vase, Peapod (H-87)	640-?	Vase, Storks, Two	808	Ashtray, Sovereign Fluted Round
488	Ashtray, Rectangular, 9" by 5"	668	Vase, Tulip, Large (H-68)	808	Ashtray, Square Moated
488	Vase, Leaves, Folded	669	Vase, Tulip, Half (H-69)	809	Ashtray
500	Vase, Urn, Tall	673	Pitcher, Wide Bottom (H-73)	810	Ashtray, Lidded
506	Vase, Pillow, Modeled	675	Vase, Cornucopia, Hand Base	810	Vase, Flame (510)

Bibliography

Henzke, Lucile. *Art Pottery of America*. Atglen, Pennsylvania: Schiffer Publishing Ltd., 1982, Revised Edition 1996.

Hoopes, Ron. *The Collector's Guide and History of Gonder Pottery, The Other Zanesville, Ohio – Art Pottery*. Gas City. Indiana: L-W Book Sales, 1992.

Reiss, Ray. *Red Wing Art Pottery*. Chicago, Illinois: Property, 1996.

Schneider, Norris F. "Lawton Gonder Began Career In Ceramics at Age of 13." Zanesville, Ohio: *Zanesville Times Signal*, September 22, 1957.

Index

Mold #550, Planter, Chinese Junk, Small, 86
Mold #551, Figurine, Oriental Man, 49
Mold #553, Planter, Horse, Winged, 86
Mold #556, Bowl, Console, w/Dolphins, 29
Mold #557, Bowl, "Banana Boat" Console, 29
Mold #559, Vase, Cuspidor, 112
Mold #561, Candleholders, Dolphin, 33
Mold #562, Vase, Two Storks, 113
Mold #565, Candleholders, Curled, 33
Mold #570, Figurine, Oriental Woman, Hands Together, 49
Mold #573, Figurine, Oriental Woman, Holding Ginger Jar, 49
Mold #581, Figurine/Lamp, Jester Head, 49
Mold #582, Bookends, Horse Head, 26
Mold #585, Planter, Twist Shoe Strap, 86
Mold #586, Ashtray, Foot Shaped, 19
Mold #587, Figurine/Lamp, Young Woman, 50
Mold #588, Figurine/Lamp, Rose Lady Head, 50
Mold #591, Dish, Leaf, Oak, 37
Mold #592, Bowl, "S" Shaped, 29
Mold #593, Planter, Nude w/Deer, 86
Mold #594, Vase, Triple "S," 113
Mold #595, Vase, Tube, Bent, 113
Mold #598, Vase, Tapered, Tall, 113
Mold #599, Vase, Leaves & Twigs, 114
Mold #603, Vase, Open Center (H-603), 131
Mold #604, Vase, Double Open Handles, 114
Mold #605, Vase, Drape, Tieback (H-605), 131
Mold #606, Pitcher, Classical, 81
Mold #607, Vase, Bulged, Square (H-607), 132
Mold #626, Ashtray, "S" Swirl, 20
Mold #662, Teapot, Beehive, Coiled, 99
Mold #668, Vase, Tulip, Large (H-68), 127
Mold #669, Vase, Tulip, Half (H-69), 127
Mold #673, Pitcher, Wide Bottom (H-73), 128
Mold #674, Planter, Basket, Slanted, 86
Mold #682, Pitcher, Two Bands, 82
Mold #683, Vase, Leaves On Branch, 114
Mold #686, Vase, Cactus, Art Deco, 114
Mold #687, Vase, Square, Curved, w/Flower, 114
Mold #688, Vase, Flower, Square, 114
Mold #690, Figurine, Two Deer, Running, 50
Mold #691, Vase, Cornucopia w/Leaves, 115
Mold #692, Planter, Cornucopia, Shell, 87
Mold #700, Planter, Rectangular, Large, 87
Mold #702, Vase, Pillow, Tapered, Rectangular, 115
Mold #703, Vase, Square Banded (E-69, E-369), 123
Mold #704, Vase, Square Footed, Large, 115
Mold #705, Vase, Square Footed, Medium, 115
Mold #706, Vase, Square Footed, Small, 116
Mold #707, Vase, Chinese, Footed Rectangle, 116
Mold #708, Vase, Rectangle, Flat, Large, 116
Mold #710, Vase, Cylinder, Small, 116
Mold #711, Planter, Footed, Double, 87
Mold #711, Vase, Cylinder, Medium, 116
Mold #712, Vase, Cylinder, Large, 117
Mold #715, Bowl, Round, Flat, 30
Mold #716, Planter, Footed, Double, 87

Mold #718, Vase, Chinese, Square, w/ Handles (537), 112
Mold #720, Vase, Chinese w/Uneven Handles, 117
Mold #724, Planter, Rectangle, Bottom, 88
Mold #726, Candleholder, Cube, 33, 117
Mold #727, Planter, Pagoda, Rectangular, 88
Mold #733, Planter, Square Flared, 88
Mold #737, Planter, Zig Zag, 88
Mold #738, Planter, African Violet, Set, 88, 89
Mold #742, Bowl, Hexagon w/Chinese Figures, 30, 89
Mold #745, Vase, Round, Small, 117
Mold #748, Planter, Flared Square, 4-Footed, Small, 89
Mold #749/20, Planter, Flared Squared "End of Day," 4-Footed, Medium, 92
Mold #750, Vase, Flared Squared, 4-Footed, Large, 117
Mold #752, Planter, Rectangle w/Round Corners, Large, 89
Mold #753, Planter, Flared Square Pedestal, 4-Footed, 89
Mold #762, Figurine, Turban Female w/Basket, 38
Mold #763, Figurine Planter, Bali Woman w/ Gourds & Top, 39
Mold #763, Figurine Planter, Bali Man w/ Gourds, 40
Mold #763, Figurine Planter, Bali Woman w/ No Top, 39
Mold #764, Figurine Planter, Indian Porters Bearing Chair, 40
Mold #765, Figurine Planters, Oriental Chair Bearers Set, 40, 41
Mold #765, Vase, Plume (539), 112
Mold #766, Figurine Planters, Basque Dancers Set, 41
Mold #771, Vase, Square Bulged (E-71), 118
Mold #772, Figurines, Fatima, 50
Mold #773, Figurine, Oriental Man Holding Jar, 50
Mold #774, Figurine, Oriental Woman Holding Open Fan, 50
Mold #775, Figurine, Oriental Man, Bearded, 51
Mold #776, Figurine, Oriental Woman, Right Hand to Head, 51
Mold #777, Figurine Planters, Oriental Water Bearers Set, Man, 42
Mold #777, Figurine Planters, Oriental Water Bearers Set, Woman, 41
Mold #779/20, Planter, Flared Rectangle "End of Day," Footed, 92
Mold #792, Planter, 2-Piece Flared Top, African Violet, 90
Mold #793, Planter, Conch Shell, Large, 90
Mold #800, Bell, Sovereign Bonnet Lady, 25
Mold #800, Planter, Racing Horse, 90
Mold #801, Urn, Sovereign Cigarette Footed, 54
Mold #802, Holder, Sovereign Fluted Cigarette, 55
Mold #802, Planter, Chuck Wagon, 91
Mold #802, Vase, Stylized Swan, 118
Mold #804, Cup, Sovereign Cigarette, 55
Mold #804, Cigarette Holders, 55
Mold #805, Ashtray, Square, 20

Mold #806, Box, Sovereign Cigarette w/Lid, 55
Mold #807, Ashtray, Round Piecrust, 20
Mold #807, Ashtrays, Sovereign Fluted Rectangular, 20
Mold #808, Ashtray, Sovereign Fluted Round, 21
Mold #811, Vase, Stylized Swan (511), 108
Mold #813, Vase, Large Double Leaf Footed (513), 109
Mold #814, Ashtray, Square w/Rounded Corners, 21
Mold #815, Ashtray, Square w/Inside Concentric Ridges, 21
Mold #816, Ashtray, Round For Stand, 22
Mold #826, Vase, Cactus (K-26), 118, 136
Mold #860, Vase, Shell Fan (J-60), 133
Mold #861, Vase, Blades of Grass, 118
Mold #862, Vase, Scroll, 119
Mold #863, Vase, Tall Flowers, Rounded Square, 119
Mold #865, Tray, Shell, 102
Mold #867, Vase, Basket Weave Knothole, 119
Mold #868, Vase, Triangular Double, 119
Mold #869, Vase, Ewer, Double Curved Handle (J-69), 134
Mold #869, Vase, Nubby Freeform, 120
Mold #871, Dish, Six-Section Relish, Large, 37
Mold #871, Dish, Six-Section Relish, Small, 37
Mold #872, Figurine, Horse Head, 51
Mold #872, Vase, Swirled "S" Handle, 4-Lips, 120
Mold #874, Figurine, Racing Horse Head, 51
Mold #876, Vase, Flared Flower, 120
Mold #901, Pitcher, Squashed, 82
Mold #902, Mug, Twisted Handle, 80
Mold #903, Cup, La Gonda Tea, 57
Mold #904, Saucer, La Gonda, 57
Mold #905, Bowl, Fruits, La Gonda, 57
Mold #907, Pitcher, La Gonda Cream, 57
Mold #908, Soup, La Gonda Handled Cream, 57
Mold #909, Mug, La Gonda Ribbon Handle, 20, 59
Mold #912, Plate, Oblong Chop, 58
Mold #913, Shakers, S&P, La Gonda, 58
Mold #914, Teapot, La Gonda, 58
Mold #915, Candleholders, La Gonda, 59
Mold #916, Snack Set, Oblong Platter, 59
Mold #916, Server, La Gonda, 59
Mold #917, Pitcher, La Gonda, 59, 60
Mold #923, Stack Set, La Gonda Creamer & Sugar, 60
Mold #924, Cookie Jar, Bulb w/Sleeping Dog Finial, 35
Mold #950, Cookie Jar, Sheriff, 36
Mold #950, Bank, Sheriff, Large, 24
Mold #952, Custard, La Gonda Covered w/ Handle, Small, 60, 61
Mold #953, Bowl, La Gonda Covered w/ Handle, Medium, 61
Mold #954, Bowl, La Gonda Covered Casserole w/Handle, Large, 61
Mold #955, Bowl, La Gonda Casserole w/Tab Handle Lid, 62
Mold #971, Strainer, Tea, 97